A STYLE MANUAL FOR AUTHORS

A STYLE MANUAL
FOR AUTHORS

EDWARD D. SEEBER

Indiana University Press
Bloomington

FOREWORD

It is the perennial hope of every American publisher that writers may somehow become more knowledgeable and painstaking in matters that affect the course of a manuscript through the usual routine of consideration, acceptance, editing, typesetting, and proofreading. At the same time it is clearly to the advantage of every author to present the kind of typescript that will obviate, as far as possible, errors, misunderstandings, delays, costly retyping, and even costlier corrections in proof—or possible rejection on the ground of slipshod preparation. In short, the demands of scholarly publication today are such that authors can no longer afford to look upon style guides as compendiums of fussy, pedantic minutiae with which they need not concern themselves.

To meet these demands, *A Style Manual for Authors* endeavors to clarify the author-publisher relationship and publishers' requirements, and to explain and illustrate acceptable principles of typescript preparation and proofreading. For maximum usefulness, and with no intention of being dogmatic, the procedures here recommended correspond in the main with the *MLA Style Sheet,* which has been influential in simplifying and regularizing the scholarly style of many American journals and university presses. The author or editor can readily adjust minor points—such as details of footnoting—to practices that are peculiar to various branches of learning or to different publishers, and appropriate allowances are made for personal choice between correct alternatives.

Other features of *A Style Manual for Authors* include

copious illustrations of footnotes and bibliography entries, foreign-language problems (titles, proper names, word division, etc.), and specimen pages showing corrections in manuscript and in galley proof. A selected bibliography lists additional works on correct usage, copyright practice, indexing, graphic methods, and special requirements in styling.

Copy handled by editors and typesetters must above all be clear, easily legible, and consistent. Esthetic appeal per se is of no importance in the manuscript; therefore, the many technicalities associated with the meticulous page design of theses and other manuscripts of permanent record are here dispensed with.*

* See Edward D. Seeber, *A Style Manual for Students,* Midland Book No. 67 (Bloomington: Indiana University Press, 1964), designed to aid in the preparation of term papers, essays, and theses.

CONTENTS

I

THE AUTHOR AND HIS PUBLISHER

1 **Author-publisher relationship.** The complex steps that lead to the production of a book or article entail certain obligations on your part, as author. If these are not understood, tolerantly accepted, and scrupulously fulfilled, awkward and unpleasant consequences will invariably result—misunderstandings, needless editorial revision, a flood of queries from your publisher to you, disruption of production schedules, errors in printing, increased costs to the publisher, substantial charges to you, and delays in publication.

Publishers' requirements can be stated broadly as follows: You will be expected to

- provide a manuscript that is carefully written, typed, styled, and corrected. Do not assume that the editor will remedy lapses and omissions, or correct any but gross and obvious errors; do not expect him to supply missing text material, verify facts, check quotations and references, guess at obscurities, and solve riddles—in short, do your work for you. Remember that the place to make corrections and alterations is in the manuscript, *not* in galley proof
- give the publisher an exclusive option on your manuscript, in fair return for his willingness to spend time and money in having the manuscript examined by his own staff and by competent outside readers. In other words, do not submit your manuscript to more than one publisher at the same time

- answer queries and meet deadlines promptly. Smooth integration of editing, production, publicity, and promotion demand strict adherence to established schedules

- furnish, and deliver in good condition, such illustrations, permissions for the use of copyrighted material, data to be used for promotion and publicity, etc., as your publisher may request

- read and correct proofs according to accepted procedures, and return them promptly

- abide by contractual agreements stipulating your obligations and the publisher's, the schedule of royalties, offer of a stated number of free author's copies, offer of your next book to the same publisher, etc.

Your publisher is somewhat like the architect who, having been informed of his client's wishes, is in the best position to decide, by virtue of his experience and superior technical knowledge, what can and what cannot be done. Your ideas about arrangement, format, typography, illustrations, and ways of promoting your book will be welcome, and you will be accommodated so far as possible; but remember that your publisher knows more than you do about these matters.

II

GENERAL SUGGESTIONS

2 Number of copies. Prepare, if possible, three copies of your manuscript—two for the publisher (who may need both for preliminary readings, promotion, etc.), and one for yourself. In any case, retain one copy as insurance against loss. If your manuscript has already been typed and you have only one or two copies, a Xerox copy may be obtained at moderate expense. All copies should be identical and contain all corrections, inserts, and other alterations.

3 Special requirements in styling. A particular publishing house or periodical for which you are writing may provide its own style guide. If not, study specimen pages and style your manuscript accordingly. Some special fields are represented below in the selected bibliography.

4 Consistency. To achieve consistency, keep before you a list of your spellings of variable proper nouns and words like *role—rôle, co-ordinate—coördinate—coordinate, theater—theatre, wilful—willful, sizable—sizeable, per cent—percent;* also forms like Mar.—March, April 1940—April, 1940, & Co.—and Co., p. 24 n.—p. 24n., Chap.—chap.—ch., etc. Note the use of required or optional capitals with words relating to religious denominations or sects, philosophical, literary, or artistic schools: Baptist, Epicurean, epicurean, Romantic Movement, romanticism, Naturalism, naturalist, Pre-Raphaelites, etc. Send a copy of this list to the publisher: it will be useful to his editor.

5 Visualizing the eventual printed form, so far as possible, will help you to space and align carefully, and to omit characters (asterisks, periods, parentheses, etc.) that are not to be so printed, and nonessential marks and flourishes. Rewrite any awkward or complicated passage that will puzzle the editor or typesetter.

6 Typography should be left to the editor and book designer. You should, of course, underline for italics and indicate desired ligatures; but do not attempt to suggest the typographical treatment of title page, table of contents, chapter and section headings, etc., and do not mark for bold face and small capitals. If you have suggestions about typography (as in the case of especially complicated material), make them in the form of a letter to your publisher.

As you write, use restraint in the employment of large capitals (which may in print appear altogether too prominent), italics (especially to convey emphasis), and exclamation marks after declarative sentences. (This does not apply to quoted matter.)

7 Anomalies in spelling, etc., that are to be so printed, are sometimes altered by a well-meaning editor. If you foresee this possibility, write in the margin (circled) "follow copy exactly."

8 Dictionaries. Editors generally follow Webster's unabridged dictionary for spelling, hyphenation, and word division. If you have instead used Funk and Wagnalls' *Standard College Dictionary,* or *Webster's New World Dictionary of the American Language* or *New Collegiate,* attach an explanatory note addressed to the editor. As you write, refer consistently to the same volume.

9 Corrections and insertions (see specimen pages 1, 2, 3). If brief, these are written (typed, if you do not write legibly) *above* the line; or they may be attached to the page with staples or paste. Do not use Scotch tape, pins, or streamers that are easily torn off and lost. Insertions in a foreign language, which the typesetter may not comprehend, should be typed. Type long insertions on separate, full-size sheets, numbering them, for example, 6a, 6b, etc. Then, at the appropriate point on page 6, write in the margin (circled) "insert pages 6a-6b here." Indicate precisely where insertions are to be made, using a caret below the line rather than a virgule (/), and revise paragraphing, footnotes, etc., as required.

Do not put corrections in the margin as you would in correcting proof: these slow up the work of the editor and typesetter, who are forced continually to shift their eyes from text to margin. Make your correction only once, simply and clearly. For example, a horizontal line through a word or a vertical line through a letter is sufficient to show deletion. (In the latter case use ligatures above and below the line, if needed, to close space.) Use vertical lines also to separate words or letters run together. If a number is to be spelled out (e.g., "17"), draw a circle around it. Periods, commas, and apostrophes, if not clear, can be marked in this way: ⊙ ⌃ ⌄.

If you delete something and then decide to retain it—assuming that it is still legible—put a row of closely spaced dots beneath ("stet" is unnecessary). If you remove an entire page, say page 11, double number the preceding page (10-11) to preserve continuity of pagination. Lesser deletions—and other corrections and alterations—do not require retyping merely for appearance' sake as long as clarity and legibility are preserved. For example, deletion of an entire sentence or paragraph does not impede legibility. But many interlinear corrections do, and in this case it is better to retype the page. (See specimen pages 2, 3.) If several lines are deleted within a paragraph, draw a line connecting the end of the preceding with the beginning of the following text (see specimen pages 1, 2).

A note or direction written in the margin should be circled.

The publisher may return your manuscript for approval after it has been edited and readied for the printer. To avoid subsequent corrections in proof, *answer all queries*. Make necessary corrections clearly and discreetly; but in no case erase anything written on the sheets by the editor. If you have questions or comments, address them separately to the publisher.

10 Copyreading. Copyread your manuscript carefully (whether you do your own typing or not), checking for accuracy and consistency in usage and style, punctuation, spacing, footnote numbering, etc. Complete all quotations and—this is most important—recheck them for correctness of source, spelling, punctuation, and accent marks. Reduce so far as possible the number of footnotes, lengthy quotations, tabulations, special characters, etc.

Remember that a seemingly minor change in galley proof may necessitate the resetting of type to the very end of the paragraph; that corrections in proof may lead to new errors, sundry difficulties, and considerable expense to you.

11 Missing or incomplete sections of a manuscript should be represented if possible by numbered pages containing appropriate headings and an estimate of the number of words or pages involved. If the length of a section cannot be predetermined, write at the foot of the preceding page "Appendix to come," etc., and attach an explanatory note. Ordinarily, however, a manuscript should be complete on delivery to the publisher.

12 Illustrations should be discussed in advance with your publisher, who will make recommendations as regards subject, finish and texture, dimensions and proportions, etc., and possibly the need for professional help in making maps, drawings, charts, etc. Do not send halftone engravings unless nothing else is available, as they do not reproduce well; photographs (glossy prints) are much preferred. Remember that maps and charts may be illegible when reduced to book-page size. You may send along any available photographs, line drawings, or rough sketches of charts and maps as a basis for further planning. On the use of copyrighted material, see below, section 54.

Identify all illustrations, giving sufficient information to enable the editor to write suitable captions, and be sure to state their source. Type such information on separate sheets, not on original photographs and drawings. Identifying numbers, etc., may be written lightly on the reverse side of photographs, taking care not to dent the paper.

13 Author's name and mailing address are typed in the upper left corner of the title page. In an article, type your name and academic address in the form and position preferred by the publisher.

14 Mailing the manuscript. For speed and safety, first-class mail (registered or certified) is best. Express or parcel post (insured) are adequate, but slower. Pages should not be bound, stapled together, folded, or bent. Paper clips may be used to separate sections. Photographs and other illustrations must be wrapped with special care as a safeguard against possible damage.

III

FORM OF THE MANUSCRIPT

15 Paper. For printer's (ribbon) copy use white, nonglossy, fairly opaque paper of standard size (8½ x 11 inches) and at least sixteen-pound weight. For clear carbon copies (one for the publisher, one for yourself) a lighter stock (e.g., thirteen-pound) is suitable. Do not use onionskin or "erasable" paper.

16 Carbon paper should be black and of good grade.

17 Type. Any standard typewriter face (elite or pica) is permissible, but use the same size throughout as an aid to the publisher in estimating length in printed pages.

18 Margins should be uniform to facilitate publisher's estimate of length, and fairly generous to allow for editorial work. A common rule is to leave approximately 1½ inches at top and left, and 1 inch at bottom and right.

19 Spacing. To facilitate correcting and editing, double space EVERYTHING—headings, text, quotations, footnotes, bibliography. Long quotations may be indicated by indention. For ordinary paragraphing, five spaces indention are sufficient.

20 Page numbers are written in the upper right-hand corner (small roman may be used for preliminary matter). Use manuscript page numbers in cross references as an aid to filling in the right numbers on page proof.

IV

THE PARTS AND THEIR FORMS

21 Parts of a manuscript are arranged in the following order:

title page	list of illustrations
dedication	list of tables
foreword	introduction
editor's preface	text
author's preface	appendix
list of abbreviations	glossary
acknowledgments	bibliography
table of contents	notes

All the common parts are here included with the exception of some (such as half titles and index) that are added after the work is in production.

Each of the above parts, and all chapters, start a new page. Notes should be typed as a separate section *at the end* of the manuscript: setting them in type is a separate operation.

22 Title page should give minimal information in any convenient form. Use capitals and lower case, and double space throughout. Omit underlining, imprint data, and matter that the editor will supply on the verso of the title page.

23 Preface (or foreword). "Foreword" sometimes denotes a brief statement written by a person other than the author; thus a book can have both a foreword and a preface. A preface, too, may be written by someone not the author. Either may be written by the author himself, in which case "fore-word" often implies relatively brief prefatory matter.

A preface (rather than an introduction, q.v.) may contain remarks concerning the purpose, limits, background, etc., of a study; editions, materials, or techniques employed; abbreviations used in text and notes (if few in number); and brief acknowledgments. Extensive abbreviations and acknowledgments may be put into separate sections.

24 **Table of contents** should include minimal data arranged to show the importance attached to the various parts of the book and their relation to each other. List all major sections (starting at left margin) with the exception of the preface or foreword. Use capitals and lower case (this will be redesigned later), and double space chapter headings and subheadings. Type manuscript page numbers at right margin as an aid to the editor.

25 **Lists of illustrations and tables** follow the general form of the table of contents. Write entries, double-spaced (including carry-over lines), in capitals and lower case. Number plates in roman capitals, figures and tables in Arabic. For specimens of form, consult published works in your field.

26 **Introduction.** An introduction, properly considered, is a part of the text and not a substitute for the preface (q.v.). It can often be dispensed with in favor of a more direct beginning in Chapter I, for which a suitable heading can be devised to show that preliminary matter is treated therein. If "Introduction" is used along with numbered headings, number it also and treat it as Chapter I.

27 **Chapter headings and subheadings** (subject to redesigning) are typed in capitals and lower case.

28 **Major subheadings** are dropped an extra space and centered on page. They may or may not be numbered. Do not underline, and omit period at end. Major subheadings may be included in table of contents.

29 **Sideheads** are dropped an extra space and typed flush with the left margin. Do not underline, and omit period at end. If these headings are clearly used for enumeration, they may be numbered in Arabic, followed by a period.

30 **Paragraph headings** (underlined, but usually not numbered) start at normal paragraph indention and are run into the paragraph. Terminate with a period—or with a period and dash (typed as two hyphens).

31 **Appendix.** Heading and title (which should always be given) are spaced like chapter headings. Label multiple appendices "Appendix A," etc., and begin each on a new page.

32 **Bibliography.** Compilation of a bibliography is treated in Chapter XIII—with no implication that every book needs one.

33 **Index.** A book may or may not need an index. If you are to make one, you will be asked to complete it within two weeks or so after receiving the necessary page proofs. (A publisher will sometimes prepare an index at the author's expense.)

Index entries can be typed in single columns on regular manuscript paper, or on suitable cards, from which the type can be set directly.

Below the heading, a note (double-spaced) may be added explaining the limitations of the index, basis of selection of items, etc.

Initial letters in subject entries may be typed either in lower case or in capitals. In the latter case, capitals will not be used in certain instances (e.g., glosses, word studies, etc.). Use commas after entry and between page references, and omit period after last page reference. Indent carry-over lines two or three spaces. Double space between carry-over lines and between entries, and leave four spaces between letters of the alphabet.

Use corrected, modernized spellings when possible, and avoid "sic." The form "Chap. IV, *passim*," may be used if appropriate, but specific page references are preferred. As shown above, words that are not index entries are underlined for italics. Write cross references as follows: Esquemeling, Alexandre, *see* Oexmelin; but write "see also *Hamlet*" without underlining. Write titles thus: *Scots Poem, A; Progress of Romance, The.* Footnotes may be indicated in various ways: 56n, 76 n. 3; 56*n*, 76 and *n.*; 39 (n. 16), 158 (nn. 38, 39).

Consult on this subject Sina Spiker, *Indexing Your Book. A Practical Guide for Authors* (Madison: University of Wisconsin Press, 1964), and the Chicago *Manual of Style.* As a general guide to form, see the index to the present volume.

V

PUNCTUATION AND THE MECHANICS
OF WRITING

34 Comma. Use a comma (*a*) before and after the abbreviations "i.e.," "e.g.," and "viz.," but not preceding "such as"; (*b*) to separate independent clauses (unless they are extremely short or have the same subject) joined by a pure conjunction (*and, but, or, for, neither, nor, yet, so*), noting that this rule concerns *clauses* so joined, not verbs (cf. "He finished the play in March and published it in April"); (*c*) to separate subordinate clauses that either precede or follow the main clause, unless they are short and closely related in thought; (*d*) in nonrestrictive clauses (those that can be omitted without changing the meaning of the main clause), e.g., "His first novel, which cost him his health, was never published" (cf. "The novel which cost him his health was his best").

In series containing three or more parts, final commas before "and" or "or" are recommended for clarity (e.g., "red, black, and blue pennants"; "the *History* was printed for Ball, Taylor, and Osborn"), notwithstanding a growing tendency to dispense with them. A comma may usually be omitted in an appositive used to distinguish its principal from other persons or things called by the same name, e.g., "the poet Young," "in his novel *Ivanhoe*"; but cf. "in her next novel, *Virginia*."

35 Hyphen. Hyphens are used mainly

• in compound numbers from twenty-one to ninety-nine

- between compound adjectival modifiers preceding nouns (e.g., a well-known man; an up-to-date process; second- and third-year courses), but not with proper nouns (e.g., a New England winter), unambiguous adverbs, especially those ending in *ly* (e.g., an ever changing scene; a hastily written essay), or modifiers that follow nouns (e.g., a man well known for his charity; a process that is up to date)

- to separate identical vowels resulting from prefixion (e.g., re-educate, supra-auditory, semi-invalid, co-ordinal; but note the present trend to write "cooperate" and "coordinate"). A dieresis over *e* or *o* may replace the hyphen (e.g., preëminent)

- to distinguish meaning (e.g., recreation, re-creation; reformation, re-formation; recount, re-count, etc.)

- in a limited number of miscellaneous compounds (e.g., D-Day, self-sufficiency, half-wit, loud-speaker, make-up, pitter-patter, un-co-operative, non-coöperation).

Bear in mind (*a*) that hyphens are optional in some words (e.g., weekend, nearby, today, goodbye); (*b*) that the trend in present-day American usage (though this is not apparent in the more traditional manuals and dictionaries) is toward fewer hyphenated words (cf. office seeker, hero worship, fellow man, cross reference, songbird, antisocial, coauthor, extralegal, nonfictional, postclassical); (*c*) that a dictionary is indispensable for guidance in the correct use of hyphens and of separate and solid words (e.g., news room, newsstand, master stroke, masterwork, water level, watermark, etc.).

36 Dash. Distinguish between a hyphen (-) and a dash (—), indicated in typing by two hyphens (- -), noting the use of the latter with dates in the sense of "to" (see section 40, line 2), and—as used here—with parenthetical remarks. Neither is preceded nor followed by a space, and a comma and dash are not used together. A four-hyphen dash (- - - -) is used where a sentence is left unfinished or ends abruptly (e.g., in dialogue), and for an omitted word or part of a word; but in proper nouns written with omitted letters, hyphens may be used to represent these letters, if known, e.g., L - - d K - - - s (Lord Kames), H - - - shire (Hampshire). If the exact word is unknown, use a prolonged dash. In titles and quoted matter, follow the original form, e.g., *Histoire de Mademoiselle de* * * * .

37 Quotation marks. Double quotation marks are preferred for general use, and single quotation marks for quotations within quotations, linguistic citations, and other limited usages. Punctuate as follows: commas and periods *precede* quotation marks, including the combination (' ") at the end of a quotation within a quotation. But with single words and phrases, and in bibliographical description, the preferred form is: *deshielo* 'thaw', "A Misreading of Poe's 'Ligeia'," "*Jalousie* appears to be a . . . form of the traditional 'psychological novel'."

Semicolons and colons *follow* quotation marks. Use care in placing question or exclamation marks in relation to quotation marks according to the sense required (e.g., He asked, "Are you coming?" Is it true that "Absence makes the heart grow fonder"?). Foreign quotation marks (e.g., French or German), which are both shaped and punctuated differently from ours, are not used with passages cited in an English text.

38 Parentheses. In parenthetical matter beginning with a capital (i.e., following terminal punctuation), the period should precede the last parenthesis. *Example*: (First edition, 1831.) In other cases, period follows. *Example*: . . . in 1840 (first published in 1831).

39 Square brackets, rather than parentheses, should enclose

• words, letters, dates, etc., interpolated by the writer within quoted matter or within titles, e.g., ". . . was a frequent visitor in his [Swift's] home"; ". . . had give[n]"; *A Trip* [in 1791] *through the Northern States*

- dates, page numbers, and other data relating to published material, lacking or incorrect in the original and supplied by the writer, e.g., [Paris], 1710; p. 149 [for 194]; [David Henshaw], *The Triumphs of Europe*

- parenthetical matter falling within parentheses. This is sometimes unavoidable, but in the commonest occurrences —e.g., (*New Verse*, XI [Oct. 1934], 8); (*The Eccentric Design* [New York, 1959], p. 10)—commas are often substituted (see section 97, sample note 28)

- phonetic transcription

- the word "sic."*

If typewriter is not equipped with brackets, they can be added neatly by hand, or improvised with virgule and underscores ($\lfloor \ \rfloor$).

40 Dates and numerals. Note the following forms: April-May, 1940; April 5, 1940—June 5, 1941; from January 1 to March 15; the 6th of July. Be consistent in using alternate forms: June 5, 1941 or 5 June 1941; June 1941 or June, 1941. If a comma precedes the year date, another follows if the sentence continues: "On June 1, 1855, he. . . ." Write "382 B.C.," but "A.D. 405," to agree with the reading "*anno Domini* 405."

Spell out (*a*) a number or date that begins a sentence, (*b*) numbers of less than three digits except dates, page numbers, connected groups (of numbers, dimensions, distances, sums of money, etc.), and numbers used in footnotes, (*c*) round

---

* "Sic" may properly be used to call attention to errors, misspellings, etc., in quoted matter—especially if these might be mistaken for typists' errors; but avoid overuse with mere archaisms, frequent misspellings in certain classes of diaries, letters, etc.

numbers (e.g., three hundred, fifteen hundred, four thousand).

Use commas in numbers having four or more digits, except in dates and page numbers. Write "the 1840's" (or "1840s"), "the forties" (but not "the 40's"), "sixteenth-century poetry" (not "16th").

Inclusive page numbers and dates may be written in full or in condensed form, e.g., 162-70, 1830-35. (The MLA *Style Sheet* allows this for dates but would have page numbers through 999 written in full.) When the first number ends in two ciphers, write the second number in full (e.g., 1600-1648); when the second last digit in the first number is a cipher, write either the final digit of the second number (e.g., 102-3, 1604-5) or the entire second number (102-103, 1604-1605). Do not write "1604-05."

41 Possessives. Formation of the possessive case in words ending in a sibilant (*s, z*) is not uniform, but the following procedures may be used for consistency: in one-syllable words, add *'s* (Keats's, Voss's, James's); in words of two or more syllables, add apostrophe but omit *s* (Dickens', Simonides', duchess', for conscience' sake), also in plural forms that add *-es* to a singular form ending in *s, sh, ch, x* or *z* (Churches', Joneses', Knoxes'). In foreign names, follow the same rule after determining whether or not the final *s* is pronounced (Solis', Mme de Genlis', Dumas's, Ninon de Lenclos's).

Avoid the possessive with titles ("*The Mill on the Floss's* conclusion") and, generally, with inanimate objects ("the academy's members," "the Tower of London's interior"), noting common exceptions ("a day's journey," "for appearance' sake," etc.).

42 Outline form (this does not apply to chapter subheadings) commonly follows this style:°

° The illustration is from an article by Harold E. Pagliaro in *PMLA*, LXXIX (1964), 45 n.

I. Expository aphorisms
II. Paradoxical aphorisms
   A. Polar paradoxical aphorisms
      1. Polar aphorisms of parallel structure
         a. parallelism of antithesis
         b. parallelism of analysis
         c. parallelism of synthesis
      2. Polar aphorisms of equational structure
      3. Polar aphorisms of comparative structure
   B. Non-Polar paradoxical aphorisms

Further divisions under *c*, above, would be introduced, in order, by (1), (a), (i), etc. Note that a minimum of two is logically required for each rank, i.e., I implies a II, 1 implies a 2, etc. A single heading is otherwise absorbed into the heading immediately preceding it.

VI

TITLES CITED IN TEXT AND IN FOOTNOTES

43 Form of title. Take book title from title page only. Take title of article from title page of article itself, not from table of contents. Add punctuation (often omitted in printed titles) as needed to avoid ambiguity or confusion, e.g., *Sidney's Appearance: A Study in Elizabethan Portraiture.* Give a title in its original form, even though it seems wrong or at variance with common practice: retain original spellings and archaisms like *Compleat, De Foe,* French *Avantures,* using "sic" only after misspellings and other errors that might appear to be your own.

Underline (to indicate italics) titles and subtitles of books (but not the Bible or books thereof), pamphlets, plays, separately published poems (regardless of length),* and periodicals. In mentioning a periodical or newspaper, one need not treat a definite article or the name of a city as part of the title (e.g., "in the *Indiana Quarterly for Bookmen*"; "in the Chicago *Tribune*"); but bibliographical citations should read *The Chicago Tribune,* etc. Enclose a title within a title in quotation marks, e.g., *Textual Studies of Goethe's "Faust."*

44 Poems, articles, theses, etc. Titles of poems not published separately, articles, chapters, sections or essays in a volume

---

* If the history of publication cannot be readily ascertained, one may italicize titles of long poems, and enclose those of short poems in quotation marks.

by several authors, and unpublished theses are enclosed in quotation marks and not underlined. Book titles that figure in such titles are underlined, e.g., "Plutarch and Rousseau's First *Discours*."

45 **Names of series** or particular editions are not underlined and need not be in quotation marks. (See section 97, sample notes 9, 10.)

46 **English titles.** Capitalize all words except prepositions, conjunctions, and articles, unless one of these is the first or the last word (the longer prepositions, like "toward," are sometimes capitalized). Capitalize any word following a colon. Usage varies as regards hyphenated compounds, and not all writers observe the Chicago *Manual of Style* rule that only nouns and proper adjectives, in the second component, are capitalized (e.g., *High-Speed Trains*; but *Fifty-first Street, English-speaking Peoples*, etc.). Hyphenated words that are considered to be one word rather than a compound are often capitalized as follows: "*If*"-*clauses, Dumb-show, the A-text, Gold-mine, Well-being, Self-scrutiny*, etc.

47 **French and Italian titles** allow great latitude as regards capitalization. Follow these acceptable rules for consistency. Capitalize an initial article, the noun following, and an adjective that may come between, e.g., *Les Femmes savantes; Le Grand Dictionnaire géographique; La Revue du mois; Studi mediolatini e volgari; Piccolo Mondo antico*. A noun used metaphorically may be capitalized, e.g., *Le Rouge et le Noir; La République des Lettres*. If a title begins with a word other than an article or an adjective, subsequent words (with the exception of proper nouns) are not capitalized, e.g., *De l'amitié; Sur la pierre blanche; Sull'oceano; Alle porte d'Italia*. See other examples below, sections 97, 111.

48 **Spanish titles.** Capitalize the first word only, e.g., *La verdad sospechosa; Amor con vista*.

49 **German titles.** Capitalize all nouns, e.g., *Zwölf mittelhoch-deutsche Minnelieder und Reimreden.* See other examples below, section 111, paragraphs 2, 3, 4, 7.

50 **Greek and Latin titles.** Capitalize the first word only, also proper nouns and adjectives based thereon, e.g., *Archivum Romanicum.* Additional capitals may be used in postclassical works, e.g., *Eikon Basilike; Pro se Defensio* (Milton); *Biographia Literaria* (Coleridge). On punctuation, see section 87.

VII

FOREIGN WORDS AND PHRASES

51 Underlining. Isolated words and phrases originating with the author are underlined if regarded as truly foreign (e.g., *aficionado, pasticcio, quatrocento, pièce à thèse, Zeitgeist*). Those already naturalized (e.g., mores, a priori, leitmotif, literati, cliché, résumé) are not underlined. The list is subject to periodic revision.*

Do not underline (*a*) quotations in a foreign language, (*b*) words or phrases quoted or used in a particular sense by an author, school, etc. (e.g., Goethe's concept of *Faust* as a "rhapsodisches Drama"), (*c*) names of foreign institutions, buildings, etc., or foreign titles preceding proper names (e.g., Opernhaus; Real Museo de Pinturas; Académie de Marseille; the Champs-Elysées; le Père Charlevoix). It follows that, except for titles within titles and a few special situations, there is no need for underlining and using quotation marks around the same word.

52 Accent marks. If your typewriter does not have foreign accent marks, add them neatly by hand (do not use typed apostrophes). Omit French and Spanish (but not Italian) accents on capitals. Supply by hand umlaut on German letters (including capitals), and the character ß if needed to reproduce quotations and titles exactly.

---

* Foreign words are no longer designated as such in some of the latest dictionaries, but they are plainly marked in *Webster's New World Dictionary of the American Language* and in the older *Collegiate* and unabridged.

53 Ligatures in Old English and foreign words are indicated by hand in the typed copy, thus: A͡Elfred; O͡Euvres; wǣter; cœur. Do not try to join the letters on the typewriter. Omit ligatures in quotations from Latin, in Anglicized derivatives from Latin, or from Greek through Latin, e.g., Aeneid, Oedipus, Caesar, subpoena, manoeuvre.

VIII

QUOTED MATTER IN TEXT

54 Permission to quote prose, verse, lyrics, or music, and to reproduce illustrations, charts, maps, etc., should be arranged with copyright owners. This is both a courtesy and a legal requirement. Remember that the period of copyright and copyright renewal runs for a total of fifty-six years. In doubtful cases, write to the Copyright Office in the Library of Congress.

Scholarly publications (books and articles) are usually copyrighted, and it is only prudent to get permission for quotations of substantial length—say, over one hundred words from any one source, or over one line of verse. Most members of the Association of American University Presses permit quoting from their publications without permission "in works of original scholarship," provided that "appropriate credit be given in the case of each quotation"; but this waiver does not extend to "quotations that are complete units in themselves (as poems, letters, short stories, essays, journal articles, complete chapters or sections of books, maps, charts, graphs, tables, drawings, or other illustrative materials."* A similar policy has been announced by the editors of some eighty scholarly journals.†

Permission for short quotations is usually given free; but a publisher may charge a fee for use of a whole chapter,

* For the complete statement see *PMLA*, LXXIX, No. 4, Pt. 1 (1964), section "For Members Only," p. A-4.
† Ibid., No. 3, p. A-4.

article, or poem. Fees are more likely to be required for material that is to be used in a textbook or anthology. If the author's book is neither, he should make this clear to the publisher from whom he is asking permission. A sample letter of request follows:

Gentlemen:

Next spring Excelsus University Press will publish my critical work entitled *The Novels of Henry James.* In this connection I request permission to quote approximately 275 words from your publication *A Life of Henry James,* by R. A. Jones, as follows:

p. 23: "James's childhood years ... his father and mother."
pp. 185-186: "One senses a conscious effort ... to the end of his life."

Yours very truly, etc.

55 **Short prose quotations** are run into the text (with double quotation marks) unless they can be typed seriatim (sometimes interspersed with longer quotations) or require special emphasis.

56 **Long prose quotations** that are to be set as separate paragraphs are dropped three spaces and *double spaced.* For clarity, indent three or four spaces from left margin. Do not use quotation marks unless they occur in the original. Triple space before resuming text. The minimum length of quotations so treated varies among publishers. For consistency you may adopt an arbitrary limit of, say, five to ten typed lines.

57 **Capitalization.** Although quotations must be scrupulously reproduced with respect to wording, spelling, and punctuation, it is common practice in some fields to alter capital and lower-case letters introducing them, e.g., "It is apparent that 'as they part, Hugh is angry ...'" ("as," in the original, was capitalized); "... summed them up thus: 'The picture which the novelist drew ...'" ("the," in the original, was not capitalized). Similarly the first word of a long quotation, introduced by a colon or following a period, may be capitalized though not so written in the original. It is correct also, in this case, to begin with the original lower-case word, preceded, at left margin, by an ellipsis sign (. . .). Use one form consistently.

58 Italics. Unless there is a special reason (as in a critical edition) for indicating the original typography, quotations from early books in which proper names, prefaces, etc., are printed in italics may be written without underlining.

59 Parenthetical references. Parenthetical source references in short prose quotations precede a final period, e.g., ". . . of his own" (p. 6). If other terminal punctuation occurs, omit period, e.g., ". . . of his own!" (p. 6) In long prose quotations set as separate paragraphs, reference follows terminal punctuation, e.g., . . . of his own. (p. 6)

60 Verse quotations of a single line may be run in the text with quotation marks unless they require unusual emphasis. Two lines may be so treated, separated by a virgule (/). Longer passages are dropped three spaces and centered on page, the margin being determined in general by the longest line. If lines are of unusual length, indent five spaces and indent carry-over lines an additional three to five spaces. (For further particulars, consult the Chicago *Manual of Style*.) Use double spacing and no quotation marks unless they occur in the original. Triple space after last line.

Line reference may, if space allows, follow the last line quoted, with no period, e.g.,

Lies buried in this lonely place. (vv. 30-32)

(The abbreviations "l.," "ll.," may also be used—handwritten to distinguish them from Arabic numbers.)

Reference to longer lines may be dropped two spaces, flush with the right-hand margin of the quoted matter. Titles, divisions, etc., are written similarly: (*Inferno*, X, 87) or (*In-*

ferno X.87), (trans. B. Q. Morgan), etc. In long citations from poems usually printed with numbered lines, use like numbers in the right margin. References to a particular volume may be omitted if the lines quoted can be found readily in various editions; but if line numbers or other details do not agree with editions usually cited (e.g., the Globe Shakespeare), the source used should be specified.

61 Ellipses at the beginning of or within a sentence or line of verse, quoted title, etc., are indicated by three spaced periods. A comma, semicolon, or colon may precede or follow the ellipsis. To indicate an ellipsis following a complete sentence, or between two sentences, use four spaced periods. Since the fourth period represents terminal punctuation, a question or exclamation mark may be substituted as required.

In extended French and Spanish texts, indicate ellipsis by three *unspaced* periods, with one space preceding and following, e.g., "La Bruyère ... soutient la même cause. ..." In Italian texts, use four unspaced periods for all ellipses, or three following a punctuation mark. No space precedes, but one space follows, e.g., "L'italiano moderno, la lingua che si studia oggi nelle scuole,... è.... una lingua convenzionale...." Do not use these patterns with incidental foreign quotations in an English text.

Show omission of one or more lines of verse or of one or more paragraphs in a long prose citation by a row of triple-spaced periods equal in length to the longest line quoted. Indicate omissions at beginning and end of verse citations as follows:

> . . . The Universal Cause
> Acts to one end . . . .

62 Paragraphing. One need not be overscrupulous about accounting for original paragraphing. A footnote reading "pp. 18, 25" may properly refer to a continuous passage quoted in the text and broken only by an ellipsis sign. Several passages may, within the bounds of intelligibility, be so treated.

63 Titles of persons, such as Mr., Dr., Professor, are commonly omitted in references to prominent authors under discussion, scholars cited, or deceased persons, though they are appropriate in more personal references, acknowledgments, etc. The titles "Miss" and "Mrs." (also omitted by some) may be replaced by a given name. Retain conventional titles with certain eminent names, e.g., Mrs. Browning, Mme de Maintenon, Dr. Johnson, Sir Walter (Scott), etc.

IX

FOOTNOTE REFERENCES IN TEXT

64 Placement. Use care in selecting the most natural and logical place for footnote reference numbers. References to quoted matter are usually put at the end of the quoted text, rather than after the author's name or an introductory phrase.

65 Numbering. In an article, including one with numbered divisions, number the notes consecutively throughout. In a book, number them consecutively by chapters. Multiple notes on technical textual matters (as in a critical edition) are placed before ordinary notes, and use as references lower-case roman a, b, c, etc., repeating after z is reached. These letters may *precede* punctuation and quotation marks. If used next to a regular footnote reference number, separate with a comma, with no spacing. In exceptional cases it is expedient to repeat the same reference number one or more times on a single page, or to use multiple references (e.g., *dervis*[a,b]), thus avoiding repetitious footnotes.

Raise footnote reference numbers in the text slightly above the line of type. Do not use parentheses. Numbers should follow punctuation and quotation marks. *Examples*: . . . papers.[2] . . . papers.)[2] . . . papers";[2] etc.

66 Symbols. The special footnote symbols *, †, ‡, §, ¶, #, especially useful after algebraic notations or wherever reference numbers would be confusing or inapt, are suitable also for articles or works like the present manual that have few footnotes. They may be used also for certain kinds of occasional footnotes in a work that has, at the same time, a number of ordinary footnotes using numerical references. These symbols may be doubled or tripled, thus providing eighteen references; but in practice few are usually needed, for they are used in sequence only on a single page, i.e., one note on page 2 and one note on page 3 will each be designated by a single asterisk.

X

FOOTNOTES

67 Effective footnoting.[*] Footnotes serve mainly to give (*a*) sources of quotations, opinions, and important facts cited in the text, and (*b*) the author's comments and explanations, additional facts, editorial and critical apparatus, technical data, etc., which, though relevant, would seem labored or distracting in the text itself. Bear in mind that footnotes result inevitably in continual (and often unrewarding) distractions to the reader, and that they should therefore be used as sparingly as is consistent with need, effectiveness, and clarity.

Avoid notes (*a*) that are not strictly relevant and essential, especially sources for facts that are of common knowledge or easily verified, (*b*) that repeat unnecessarily the substance of previous notes or textual matter, (*c*) that may be combined with adjacent notes (often accomplished effectively by rewording the text, rearranging material, or grouping several consecutive references), (*d*) that can be replaced in the text by short, parenthetical references to works frequently cited,[†]

---

[*] The following procedures apply generally both to notes printed on the page (as they appear in journal articles and in some books) and to those placed at the back. The latter arrangement, where successive notes to several pages are usually brought together on a single sheet, permits slight modifications such as those indicated in sections 72, 90-92.

[†] Avoid overextending this practice to references that belong properly in footnotes. Notes in the text proper must not distract the reader or suggest that two discrepant systems of footnoting are in use.

also by remarks like "italics added,"* (e) that are overlong: many long notes can be eliminated or at least shortened by adding information in the text, (f) that are of extreme length or complexity (such matter, if indispensable, may be put into one or more appendices or in the bibliography).

Use cross references sparingly; usually they should point forward rather than back.

A source reference usually precedes a quotation or remark introduced by the author's name or its equivalent; if not so introduced, it may follow. (See section 97, sample footnotes 27-34.)

68 Typing footnotes. Type all notes separate from text, with the exception of notes to tables, which should go beneath the tables. Indent the first line of a note five spaces, and *double space* throughout. Number notes in Arabic, on line of type, followed by a period.

69 Prose citations several lines or paragraphs in length are not dropped two spaces, but are run in the text of the footnote, with quotation marks at beginning and end. Intervening paragraphs begin, but do not end, with quotation marks.

70 Verse citations of one or two lines may be run in the text of a footnote; otherwise, center lines on page and omit quotation marks. Leave three spaces before and after. Source may be indicated parenthetically two spaces below the last line, ending approximately below the last letter of the longest line quoted.

71 First references to published books and articles should give all pertinent bibliographical details. As an aid to the reader, repeat this form at the first recurrence of the reference in succeeding chapters. The remainder of this chapter shows the correct order of details, subject to possible omissions consistent with the form and sense of a given note.

* Use italics for emphasis as little as possible in text and in quoted matter.

72 Author's name is written with given name or initials first, and is followed by a comma. Give the fullest form used in the work cited, omitting abbreviations representing degrees, etc. In a work that has no bibliography, replace a first initial, if possible, by a given name as an aid to the reader. In the case of prominent authors (e.g., Dante, Voltaire, Goethe, T. S. Eliot), initials and single or simplified names may be used in the text and footnotes, and amplified, if desirable, in the bibliography.

If a work has several authors, give the first name, followed by "and others" or "et al." (All the names may be given if there are no more than three.) A pseudonym, when first used, may be followed by the author's real name, in brackets. For anonymous works of known or conjectured authorship, enclose the name in brackets. In the latter case, insert a question mark before the last bracket, e.g., [Daniel Defoe?].

Avoid repeating authors' names unnecessarily in footnotes. If "Max Fuchs" is cited in the text, the volume reference in the note should begin with the *title*. If the textual reference is merely "Fuchs," the note may begin with the full name, "Max Fuchs," although it may be preferable to give the full name in the text. In subsequent references, "Fuchs" alone is sufficient if no other author with the same surname is cited. In notes placed at the back of a book, a freer use of authors' full names will aid the reader.

73 French names. A hyphen is regularly used between given names: M.-J. Chénier stands for Marie-Joseph Chénier; but M. R. Canat (a form found now and then on title pages) stands for Monsieur René Canat. The particle *de* may be used following a given name, but not with the last name alone (Alfred de Vigny; Vigny; but *not* de Vigny). The same applies to German *von* or *van* and to Dutch *van der*, etc. Some names of recent date (e.g., De Gaulle; Von der Mühll) are exceptions. For additional examples see section 106.

74 Spanish names are sometimes used in the full paternal-plus-maternal form (Ortega y Gasset), but more often a name will have contracted to the paternal form alone (Juan de Valdés) or to the paternal-maternal form without the conjunction (Blasco Ibáñez). Particles are treated as in French (Valdés is correct, not de Valdés). If, in a compound paternal name, the first name is "weak," i.e., commonplace and undistinguished (this includes most names in -*ez*, and the name García), the *last* name is often used in general reference, e.g., Pedro López de Ayala may be called Ayala (or by the full paternal name López de Ayala), but not López. Similarly, in a combined paternal-maternal name that has a "weak" paternal name, the maternal name may be used in general reference, e.g., Federico García Lorca may be referred to as Lorca (or by the full name García Lorca), but not as García.

Foreign names are discussed further in sections 106-8.

75 Multiple references. If a footnote contains references to several authors or titles, separate these with semicolons, e.g., Smith, p. 10; Jones, p. 2.

76 Names of institutions, societies, agencies, etc., as given on a title page, may appear as author. See section 97, sample note 5, and section 111, paragraph 9.

77 Title should be given the first time in full, or, if extremely long, in clearly abridged form, usually after the first few words. If the complete title appears later in a bibliography, use appropriate ellipsis signs, which you may discard in subsequent notes. After the first citation, title may be further simplified. Completeness of citation will depend on the nature and requirements of the study. A first citation, if there is no bibliography, may read: [Daniel Defoe], *The Life, Adventures, and Pyracies, of the Famous Captain Singleton* . . . (the remainder of the title—over one hundred words—being omitted); if there is a bibliography: *The Life . . . of . . . Captain Singleton;* and, in subsequent citations, *Life of Singleton.* (See also above, Chapter VI, "Titles Cited in Text and in Footnotes.") Title is followed by a comma unless the next detail is in parentheses.

If a chapter of a book or part of a volume by several authors is cited, it is enclosed in quotation marks (not underlined), followed by a comma and often by the word "in" preceding the volume title (see section 97, sample notes 11, 12). Chapter titles in books are rarely cited.

A footnote to a passage containing a title should not repeat that title verbatim or in abridged form (see section 97, sample note 1); but an abridged title in the text may be expanded in a footnote.

78 **Editor's, compiler's, or translator's name** is given in normal order, preceded by "ed.," "comp.," or "trans.," and followed by a comma unless the next detail is in parentheses. If particular reference is made, not to the text, but to an editor's or translator's technique, critical remarks, etc., this name may come first in the reference, followed by a comma and "ed." or "trans." In this case, title of the work comes next, followed by a comma, the word "by," and the author's name. (See section 97, sample notes 6, 8, 9, 11, 13-15.)

79 **Edition used,** if not the first, is indicated in abbreviated form: 4th ed., rev. ed., new ed., etc. A comma follows unless the next detail is in parentheses. (See section 97, sample notes 4, 19.)

80 **Series name** or that of a particular edition may be omitted in a footnote if it occurs in the bibliography. Name is not underlined, and quotation marks or parentheses need not be used unless you are following a particular style. A comma follows unless the next detail is in parentheses. (See section 97, sample notes 9, 10.)

81 **Number of volumes,** usually omitted when reference is to specific volume(s) or if this detail is given in the bibliography, is written with Arabic number followed by "vols." and a comma, unless the next detail is in parentheses. (See section 97, sample note 2 and remark.)

82 Place of publication, publisher, date are written within parentheses followed by a comma.* These items, together with edition and page reference, may be omitted singly or in combination in references to well-known and frequently edited poems and plays (e.g., *The Deserted Village;* works by Shakespeare or O'Neill), also in standard reference works (encyclopedias, dictionaries, *DNB*, etc.). Facts of publication (place, publisher, date) may be omitted, in an article or chapter, after the first citation, unless they serve a particular purpose.

83 Place of publication. For clarity and to avoid ambiguity, place name may be identified by country or state:

> Göteborg, Sweden
> Bloomington, Ind.: Principia Press
> Bloomington: Indiana Univ. Press
> Cambridge, Mass., 1935
> Cambridge: Cambridge Univ. Press

It is often correct to list more than one place of publication (Boston & New York: Houghton Mifflin Co.) or to indicate joint publication (New York: The Modern Lang. Assoc. of America; London: Oxford Univ. Press). In some cases one place suffices (Chicago: Scott, Foresman & Co., omitting their offices at Atlanta, Dallas, and New York, though given on title page; New York: Holt, Rinehart & Winston, omitting Toronto and London if the book was printed in the United States).

Writers sometimes Anglicize foreign places of publication (Turin, Munich, The Hague, etc.), but in works dealing with European literature, or requiring more precise bibliographical description, original spellings are often preferred (To-

---

* For alternate forms when entire reference, including title, is in parentheses, see section 97, sample note 28 and remark.

rino, München, La Haye, Genève, Londres, Francofurti, Oxonii, etc.).

Place of publication is followed by a colon if publisher's name is given, or by a comma if followed directly by the date. If place is not given on title page, supply it in brackets if known.* If unknown, write "n.p."

84 Publishers' names often provide essential information, as in the case of a title printed in the same year or in the same city by two or more publishers. Sometimes they are given in titles of recent date and, in the same manuscript, omitted in those presumably out of print. (The dividing date is arbitrary: one may include publishers of works printed within, say, the last twenty years, or within the copyright period of fifty-six years.) Or, they may be omitted in footnotes if they occur later in the bibliography. Some publishers of books and scholarly journals (e.g., *PMLA*) prefer to omit them altogether.

Names should be simplified: instead of "Librairie académique Perrin et Cie, libraires-éditeurs," write "Perrin et Cie," or simply "Perrin"; "Macmillan & Co." may be written "Macmillan." (Note use of ampersand and abbreviation "Co.") Further abbreviation (e.g., New York Univ. Press) is common in some fields but not in others.

85 Date is given in Arabic numerals even if original is in roman. If date is not given on title page or in copyright notice (usually on verso of title page), supply it, if known, in brackets. If unknown, write "n.d." If conjectured, put a question mark before last bracket or write "c. 1932," etc. (See various specimens in sample notes and in bibliographical section, and additional remarks in the next two sections.)

---

* But avoid the pedantic use of brackets when the place is clearly implied: if "Hachette" alone appears on title page, write "Paris: Hachette," without brackets, unless a more formal description is in order.

86 Articles. The full title, in quotation marks, is followed by a comma, the name of the periodical (underlined and often abbreviated), a comma, the volume number (in roman capitals), the date (in parentheses), a comma, and the pagination, omitting "p." or "pp." Place of publication may be added in exceptional cases for clarification, e.g., *Hispania* (Madrid). For recent issues, the precise month or number may be included: (Nov., 1963), (Spring, 1963), in which the commas are optional; IV, No. 2 (1963) or IV, 2 (1963), though once a periodical is bound by volumes this detail usually serves no purpose. Dates *must* be so written if the periodical does not have consecutive pagination throughout the year (see section 97, sample notes 22, 23). If a periodical is published in more than one series, series number must be included, e.g., *The Library*, 5th ser., XV (March 1960), 10. The designation may also be Old Series or New Series (O.S., N.S. or, commonly, o.s., n.s.), sometimes placed before the volume number, sometimes after, e.g., *The American Monthly Magazine*, n.s., I (1836) or I, n.s. (1836).

For articles in newspapers and weeklies, give date, section number, page, and column, as needed, omitting volume number. (See section 97, sample notes 20, 25.)

87 Volume and page numbers. Write the former in roman capitals, the latter in Arabic (except when small roman is used for prefaces, etc.). The correct form for a work of more than one volume is III, 28-31, omitting "Vol." and "pp." (For exceptions, see title in next paragraph and section 97, sample notes 5, 7, 11.) In Greek and Latin works, comma may be omitted after both author and title. Note spacing and use of periods in the following: Cicero *De amicitia* XXVII.101; Plato *Republic* 546A; and, in biblical references, Judges XIX. 27-28 (or 19:27-28). Plays, works divided into cantos, etc., may be written similarly (e.g., *Macbeth* V.iii.22; *Inferno* X.87) or, more conventionally, *Macbeth*, V, iii, 22, etc.

The date of a particular volume of a work published over a period of years can, if desired, be shown thus: *The Letters of Sir Walter Scott*, VI (London, 1934), p. 8—*not* (London, 1934), VI, 8, for here the correct date would be 1932-37, that of the *edition*. A shorter form of this reference, when place is omitted, may be written thus: VI (1934), 8. (See section 97, sample notes 6, 7.)

In citing a single-volume work, and otherwise when no volume number is given, write "p. 11," "pp. 28-31," "Ibid., p. 5," etc. Note also: p. 28, n. 2; III, 28, n. 2. Page numbers cited from the same volume are separated by commas (e.g., pp. 2, 14, 34), references from different volumes by semicolons (e.g., I, 3, 5; II, 45).

An alternate system of notation, used in the *Readers' Guide to Periodical Literature* and in certain types of publication, gives first the volume number (in Arabic), then the pagination, then the date, as follows: *American Journal of Sociology*, 58:359-360, 1953. Use only when admissible in your field.

XI

ABBREVIATIONS AND LATINISMS IN FOOTNOTES

88 Underlining. Note that the Latinisms below are not underlined for italics: this accords with the trend encouraged by the *MLA Style Sheet*.

89 Ibid. (for *ibidem*, "in the same place") is used to repeat *as much as possible* of a reference in the note immediately preceding:

5. Smith, *Works*, IV, 55.
6. Ibid., II, 21 (*not* "Smith, ibid., II, 21").
7. Ibid., p. 30 (*not* "Ibid., II, 30").
8. Ibid.

Do not use "ibid." if the note preceding contains more than one title.

90 Op. cit. (for *opere citato*, "in the work cited"), referring to one of several titles cited in a note immediately preceding or (usually) to a title in an earlier note, has fallen into some disfavor, for its overuse easily results in ineffectual pedantry. If an author's name appears in the text, a footnote reference "Op. cit., p. 5" is correct, although the simpler form "p. 5" suffices and is even preferable in annotating a compact series of quotations from the same work. If the author's name is not given or plainly inferred from the text, the form "Pope, p. 5" is recommended (here an added "op. cit." is clearly redundant).

If notes are to be printed on the page, do not force the reader, by a careless use of "op. cit." or notes like "Pope, p. 5," to search back more than a page or two for the title in question; instead, repeat the title or use a short title (see section 97, sample notes 3, 7, 8). *Check this point carefully in your manuscript.* Do not use "op. cit." to refer to a title cited in a previous chapter, or to repeat the title of a periodical when reference is to another author.

91 **Loc. cit.** (for *loco citato*, "in the place cited") may be used with or without the author's name to repeat an entire reference. It should not substitute for "ibid.," should not be followed by a page reference (here the author's name or "op. cit." would be used), and should not refer to a previous "loc. cit.," when notes are printed on the page, unless the full citation appears on the same or preceding page. *Example*:

16. Paul Nettl, "Goethe and Mozart," in *Goethe Bicentennial Studies*, p. 83.
17. Thomas, p. 3.
18. Nettl, loc. cit.

Titles must be used rather than "op. cit." or "loc. cit." when more than one work by a given author has been cited.

92 **Idem** ("the same") is a time-honored but now relatively little-used device for repeating an author's name. It is just as easy—and clearer—to repeat the name itself. If used in notes that go on the page, "idem" should refer only to matter on the same or preceding page.

93 **Passim and cf.** Use "passim" sparingly: specific page references are preferable. Avoid the use of "cf." (for *confer*, "compare") when "see" is intended.

94 **Abbreviating titles, etc.** Titles, editions, manuscripts, libraries, and (occasionally) authors cited many times may be abbreviated or otherwise simplified by symbols, key letters, etc., provided that your preface or an early footnote explains the method followed. (See section 97, sample notes 17, 18.) Periodical titles, especially those familiar in a particular field, are commonly abbreviated (e.g., *N&Q* for *Notes & Queries*; see list preceding the annual bibliographical number of *PMLA*). In a work that contains titles that the reader will possibly not comprehend in abbreviated form, it is well to write full titles the first time cited. Often it suffices to use abbreviations in the footnotes, and full titles in the bibliography. If the number of journals is large, or if abbreviations have to be devised, insert an explanatory list after the preface, or even at the beginning of the bibliography if abbreviations are used there also.

95 Some common abbreviations. Note the form, spacing, punctuation, and capitalization of the following:

abr. (abridged; abridgment)
Act IV, sc. iv (or Sc. II in a play not divided into acts)
A.M. or a.m.
anon. (anonymous)
art., arts. (article, articles)
b. (born)
biog. (biography, biographer, biographical)
Bk. VI, Bks. VI, IX
c. or ca. (*circa*, with dates; do not use in sense of "copy-righted")
Chap. VI (or, occasionally, vi), Chaps. VI-VII (or, occasionally, chap., chaps.; ch., chs.)
col., cols. (column, columns)
comp. (compiler, compiled by)
d. (died)
diss. (dissertation)
ed., eds. (edition, editions; editor, edited by)
ed. cit. (edition cited)
esp. (especially, as in "see esp. Chap. II")

fac. or facsim. (facsimile)

fasc. (fascicle)

fig., figs. (figure, figures)

fl. (*floruit*, he or she flourished)

fol., fols. or foll. (folio, folios)

illus. (illustration; illustrated)

l., ll. (line, lines, either spelled out or hand-written to avoid confusion with numerals)

MS, MSS (MS takes a period when referring to a specific manuscript, e.g., MS. D)

n., nn. (note, notes)

n.d. (no date)

n.p. (no place)

n.s., or, less often, N.S. (new series; capitalize for New Style)

No. 6

o.s., or, less often, O.S. (old series; capitalize for Old Style)

p., pp.; pp. 25 f. (or, better, pp. 25-26; pp. 25, 26); pp. 25 ff. (i.e., p. 25 and several pages following; inferior sometimes to notation of exact pages)

par., pars. (paragraph, paragraphs)

pl., pls. (plate, plates)

Pt., Pts., pt., pts. (part, parts)

pub. or publ., pubs. (published; publication, publications)

rev. (revised, revised by; review, reviewed by)

s.v. (*sub verbo* or *voce*, "under the word——")

Sec., Secs., sec., secs. (section, sections)

ser., or, less often, Ser. (series)

sig., sigs. (signature, signatures)

sig. C5^r or 5r (recto), 5^v or 5v (verso)

st., sts. (stanza, stanzas)

trans. or tr. (translator, translated by)

Vol. X, Vols. X-XI

vs. or v. (versus)

vs., vss., or v., vv. (verse, verses)

American writers often prefer the following forms to the alternatives given in parentheses:

above (supra; ante)
and others (et al.)
below (infra; post)
ff. (et seq.)
n.d. (s.d., for *sine die*)
n.p. (s.l., for *sine loco*)
see (vide)
to wit (sc. or scil., for *scilicet*)

96 Beginning of note. At the beginning of a footnote or sentence, some writers prefer "Page," "Pages," "Line" "Lines," etc., to "P.," "Pp.," "L.," "Ll.," etc., as being more pleasing to the eye.

XII

SAMPLE FOOTNOTE REFERENCES

97 Sample footnotes. The following footnotes illustrate various points covered above.

  [1] Norman L. Torrey, *The Spirit of Voltaire* (New York: Columbia Univ. Press, 1938), p. 58. [If both author's name and title appeared in the text, the note would begin with the first parenthesis: (New York, etc.)]

  [2] John Morley, *Diderot and the Encyclopaedists*, 2 vols. (London: Macmillan, 1897). ["New York" might be added; but this edition was printed in England. In a commoner type of note, followed by a page reference, "2 vols." would normally be omitted; but if needed, the note would then read: . . . *Encyclopaedists* (2 vols.; London: Macmillan, 1897), I, 10]

  [3] *Diderot*, II, 73-75. [Short-title form of citation in n. 2]

  [4] [Noël-Antoine Pluche], *Histoire du ciel* . . . , 2nd ed. (Paris, 1740), I, 80. [Anonymous work. Abridged title might be expanded if not given later in bibliography]

  [5] Smithsonian Institution, *Smithsonian Treasury of Science*, ed. Webster P. True (New York: Simon & Schuster, [1960]), I, 40.

  [6] Shelley, *Complete Works*, ed. R. Ingpen & W. E. Peck (New York, 1926-30), IV (1928), 73. [Rather full form, suggesting first reference in notes. Volume date usually omitted]

  [7] Shelley, *Works*, IV (New York, 1928), p. 73. [Simplified form, again specifying date of a particular volume. Note use of "p."]

[8] *Works*, ed. Ingpen & Peck, IV, 73. [The same, further simplified]

[9] Jean de La Bruyère, *Œuvres*, ed. Servois, Les Grands Ecrivains français (Paris, 1912), I, 3. [Work in a series]

[10] John Robert Moore, *Defoe's Sources for "Robert Drury's Journal,"* Indiana Univ. Publications, Humanities Series No. 9 (Bloomington: Indiana Univ., 1943), pp. 22-23. [Title within title; work in a series]

[11] William F. Bottiglia, "Voltaire's *Candide*: Analysis of a Classic," in *Studies on Voltaire and the Eighteenth Century*, ed. Theodore Besterman, Vol. VII (Genève: Institut et Musée Voltaire, 1959), p. 8. [This, and n. 12, represent individual contributions in a series or volume by various authors]

[12] Frank E. Farley, "The Dying Indian," in *Kittredge Anniversary Papers* (Boston, 1913), pp. 251-53. ["In" may be omitted here, also in n. 11]

[13] Joseph Addison, *Works*, ed. Tickell (London, 1721), I, xii. [Usual reference to an author's edited works. Cf. the next note]

[14] Thomas Tickell, ed., *Works*, by Joseph Addison (London, 1721) . . . . [Here the reference concerns the editor's contribution rather than Addison's writings. If both figure in several references, use the form shown in n. 13]

[15] Otis E. Fellows and Norman L. Torrey, eds., *The Age of Enlightenment: An Anthology of Eighteenth-Century French Literature* (New York: Crofts, 1942), p. 21. [Or, F. S. Crofts & Co. Colon and hyphen added in title. Cited in later notes as *Age of Enlightenment*]

[16] Margaret L. Pflueger, "The Influence of Montaigne on Rousseau's First *Discourse*" (diss., Ohio State Univ., 1941), p. 3. [Quotation marks with unpublished material]

[17] Bibliothèque Inguimbertine de Carpentras (hereafter called Carp.), MS. 1871, fol. 81.

[18] Carp. 1871, fol. 111. [Simplified form of n. 17]

[19] *Encyclopaedia Britannica*, 13th ed., art. "Paper." [Standard works require minimal publication data. An alternate, more explicit form: "Paper," *Encyclopaedia Britannica*, 13th ed., XIX, 725 (or, Vol. XIX, omitting page number). If author's name is important, such a reference may begin: Thomas Babington Macaulay, "Goldsmith, Oliver," etc. References to editions after the 14th (1929), which are unnumbered, may be written thus: (Chicago, 1961), V, 25]

[20] Chicago *Tribune*, Nov. 10, 1943, p. 24, col. 4. [Standard newspaper reference. See also n. 25]

[21] E. E. Stoll, "Symbolism in Coleridge," *PMLA*, LXIII (1948), 263. [Standard periodical reference]

[22] William R. Parker, "Report of the Delegate to the American Council of Learned Societies," *PMLA*, LXXIII (April 1958), 30. [Unlike the regular issues, this April (bibliographical) number has separate pagination, therefore the month is added. Cf. the next two notes]

[23] *Atlantic Monthly*, CCXI (June 1963), 64.

[24] *Deutsche Zeitung*, V (Oct. 4, 1950), 5.

[25] *Time*, Mar. 17, 1947, p. 59. [The commoner weeklies, like newspapers, are usually cited without volume number, and parentheses are omitted around dates]

[26] Desfontaines, *Le Nouveau Gulliver* (1730), as quoted in Leonora C. Rosenfield, *From Beast-Machine to Man-Machine* (New York: Oxford Univ. Press, 1941), p. 183.

[27] R. M. Smith, "Three Interpretations of *Romeo and Juliet*," *South Atlantic Bulletin*, XXIII (1948), 60-77, after summarizing three "conflicting interpretations" which prevail among critics, rejects them one by one and concludes: "Do we . . . ?" [Illustrates source placed at beginning of note. See n. 28 for interpolated reference enclosed in parentheses; also nn. 29, 30]

[28] C. D. Locock (*Poems of Shelley*, London, 1911, II, 280, 529), following Mrs. Shelley's second collected edition (1839), prints them as two. [Also correct, though more troublesome: C. D.

Locock (*Poems of Shelley* [London, 1911], II, 280, 529), etc. Similarly, a periodical reference in parentheses may be written: (... *FR*, XXXVI, 1963, 459)]

[29] He states (p. 10) that he had "heard rational men . . . ."

[30] In III, 9, he says: "London was . . . ."

[31] "Soon after his return in 1842, he was tried by a Court Martial . . ." (*DNB*).

[32] And perhaps editor-in-chief, if that is what Boswell's "engaged . . . to superintend" means (Hill-Powell, I, 307). [Or, . . . means. Hill-Powell, I, 307. Follow one style consistently. Although references in nn. 31 and 32 are put at the end (the less awkward position), the form shown in nn. 27-30 is generally preferred if practicable]

[33] ". . . a high degree of taste . . ." (ibid., p. 5).

[34] ". . . a high degree of taste . . . ." (Ibid., p. 5.) [In the last two examples, note the change in ellipsis sign, capitalization, and closing period. In n. 34, parentheses may be omitted (see n. 32, remark). Follow one style consistently]

XIII

BIBLIOGRAPHY

98 Need of a bibliography is mainly a question of utility to the reader and appropriateness. Scholarly works often require the listing of titles related to the subject treated; and some semischolarly and even popular books can justifiably provide source references and guides to further reading. But there are scholarly books that need no bibliographies—for example, interpretive essays based on standard editions that can readily be introduced in the preface or in occasional footnotes. Or, a book that cites relatively few sources can let the footnotes themselves function as bibliography; but this device must be handled discreetly, for notes that are overloaded with titles are both difficult to read and quite unsuitable for reference purposes.

99 Heading. Since relatively few studies offer in the bibliography section an exhaustive list of works by a given author, or on a given subject, the heading "Bibliography" may be both overpretentious and inaccurate. Choose therefore a more precise heading such as "Works Cited," "List of References, Partially Annotated," "Selected List of References," "Selected Bibliography," "Sources Consulted," etc. Heading may be followed directly by a statement (double-spaced and running from left to right margins) explaining abbreviations, omissions, and other special features.

100 Contents. For easy reference, all entries—primary and secondary printed sources, journals, occasional manuscripts—

can usually be put in a single section; but a separation of disparate material (printed and manuscript sources, public documents, news articles, editorials, reports, decrees, etc.) is sometimes desirable, especially if the number of items is large. Another common division consists of works about an author, and works by the author. Division headings (if any) are centered on page, the important words capitalized (*not* underlined), with triple spacing before and after. They need not be numbered.

101 Annotation. Brief annotations enhance the value of many bibliographies. See section 111, entries Sainte-Beuve in paragraph 3 and Weintraub in paragraph 7, also the several volumes of Cabeen (ed.), *A Critical Bibliography of French Literature* (Syracuse University Press), the source of these examples.

102 Form. Begin each entry at left margin, indent subsequent lines of the same entry from three to five spaces, and double space throughout.

Special forms of bibliographies, such as numbered entries placed at the end of the volume or after sections or chapters, are familiar to readers in certain fields and may be employed if appropriate.

To economize in space and printing cost, the larger bibliographies (like Cabeen, above), usually adopt patterns of styling that deviate radically from the normal.

103 Author's name. Give the fullest form of the author's name used in the work listed. If possible, replace initials by given names as an aid to the reader. If desired, title-page form can be represented exactly thus: Smith, A[bner] B. If a work is signed only with initials, enter these in lieu of full name, e.g., enter A.B.S. under S., A.B., or, if name is known, S[mith], A[bner] B.°

° In a bibliographical listing do not supply a given name (except in brackets) if the Library of Congress card gives initials only (e.g., Thomas, T A). Such cards are catalogued separately, ahead of those bearing given names.

The completeness of the author entry is at the discretion of the writer. Under certain circumstances it would seem pedantic to supply the given names of, say, T. S. Eliot or H. G. Wells, or the real names of familiar writers like Anatole France, Novalis, Owen Meredith, or Gorki. Also, it would be misleading to list the well-known "Eugène" Sue under his real name, Marie-Joseph Sue.

104 Anonymous authors; pseudonyms. In anonymous works, any intimation of authorship on title page should be included (see section 111, paragraph 10, sample entries *Literary Amusements* and *Le Mari silphe*). Enter anonymous works of known or presumed authorship as follows: [Defoe, Daniel], or [Defoe, Daniel?]. Enter pseudonymous works thus: Tallentyre, S. G., pseud. of Evelyn Beatrice Hall; or, Tallentyre, S. G. [Evelyn Beatrice Hall].

105 Repeated name. To repeat an author's name, type a solid line from five to seven spaces long, starting at left margin and ending with a period. Arrange titles by a single author alphabetically (including collected works, contrary to usual library cataloguing system) unless there is good reason for choosing a chronological order. Both styles should not be used in the same section. If there are one or more titles by Arnold B. Smith, and another by the same Smith in collaboration with Tracy R. Jones, enter this title last as follows: ————, and Tracy R. Jones. (Or, Jones, Tracy R. See section 111, paragraph 5, third entry and remark.) This would be followed by works by Smith and *two* collaborators, etc. In listing like names, the simpler forms precede the more complex: Jones, John, precedes Jones, John Thomas.

106 French names are alphabetized as follows:

La Place, Antoine de
Maupassant, Guy de
Montesquieu, Charles de Secondat, Baron de

In some cases the particle *de* plus the article have become affixed to the name (e.g., Du Guesclin; Des Barreaux). More recent names (e.g., De Gaulle) sometimes begin with the particle, as do Anglicized forms like De la Mare; De Selincourt.

107 **Spanish names** in their full form consist of given name (José) plus paternal name (Ortega) plus conjunction (y) plus maternal name (Gasset). While this form is usual in some instances, most names drop the conjunction and the maternal name (e.g., Lázaro Cárdenas; Juan de Valdés; Pedro Calderón de la Barca). Another common simplification consists in dropping only the conjunction, thus bringing together the paternal and maternal names (e.g., Vicente Blasco Ibáñez; Manuel Avila Camacho). As a general rule, alphabetize Spanish names by the paternal name only, treating particles in the same way as the French particle *de*. The foregoing names would be listed as follows:

> Avila Camacho, Manuel
> Blasco Ibáñez, Vicente
> Calderón de la Barca, Pedro
> Cárdenas, Lázaro
> Ortega y Gasset, José
> Valdés, Juan de

Names like José Léon Toral, Estéban Manuel de Villegas, and Carlos Antonio López cannot be alphabetized correctly until one determines whether the second name is the paternal name, or a second given name. In a combined paternal-maternal name like Federico García Lorca, having a "weak" paternal name (explained above, section 74), the maternal name (Lorca) is used so commonly for general reference that in bibliography and indexing it is well to use cross references: Lorca. *See* García Lorca.

108 **German and Dutch names.** German names written with an umlaut (*ä, ö, ü*) are listed as though spelled out (*ae, oe, ue*). In German and Dutch names, treat *von, van, van't,* and *van der* like the *de* in Guy de Maupassant (e.g., Spee, Friedrich von), noting exceptions (Von der Mühll, Emanuel; Enno van Gelder, H. A.).

For further guidance, consult foreign encyclopedias, Library of Congress cards, Chicago *Manual of Style* (section "Indexes"), and Sina Spiker, *Indexing Your Book* (Madison: University of Wisconsin Press, 1964).

109 Details. The amount of bibliographical detail required in an entry will be determined by the nature of the study. It is usually unnecessary to enter excessively long titles, the format (fol., 8vo, etc.), authors of prefaces, or the pagination of books. Articles, however, show complete pagination as well as continuations in later numbers or volumes (see section 111, entry Henderson in paragraph 12). In a bibliography containing many titles published in one place, the name may be omitted if so explained at the outset, e.g., "Place of publication is Paris unless otherwise noted." Except in special cases, record the total number of volumes in a multivolume work rather than particular volumes cited in footnotes. (Cf., in section 111, paragraph 3, entries Channing and Sainte-Beuve; paragraph 4, entries Mirabeau and Voltaire.)

In a bibliography entry, retain the same order of details as prescribed above for footnote references; but list the author's last name first, and use periods rather than commas to separate the main parts of the entry, i.e., author, title (book or article), and facts of publication. Omit parentheses with the latter. Supply missing data (author, place, date, etc.) in brackets, if determinable, and add question marks in cases of conjecture.

Enter anonymous works under their titles, not under a section labeled "Anonymous." Retain initial articles in titles, but alphabetize under the next word, e.g., list *A Voyage . . .* under

V. In foreign works, English "ed.," "trans.," "vols.," etc., may be used instead of their foreign equivalents. Foreign places of publication are discussed above, section 83. For further technical discussion, see Ronald B. McKerrow, *An Introduction to Bibliography for Literary Students* (Oxford: Clarendon Press, 1928), and Fredson Bowers, *Principles of Bibliographical Description* (New York: Russell & Russell, 1962).

110 Checking. As a final and most important step, compare each title cited in your footnotes with the corresponding entry in the bibliography. Failure to do so will invariably result in omissions, discrepancies, and errors in various details.

XIV

SAMPLE BIBLIOGRAPHY ENTRIES

111 Sample bibliography entries. The following examples illustrate common types of bibliographical entry and their styling.

1. Edited or translated works:

Dante Alighieri. *The Divine Comedy of Dante Alighieri,* trans. J. A. Carlyle, Thomas Okey, and P. H. Wicksteed; Introd. by C. H. Grandgent. The Modern Library. New York: Random House, 1932. [Less formally, "Dante," since "Alighieri" recurs in title. Grandgent's introduction is included because of this scholar's eminence in Dante studies]

Dictionary of Political Economy, ed. R. Palgrave. 3 vols. New York: Macmillan, 1901-8. [Or, Sir Robert Palgrave, although the simpler form serves its purpose here]

Fordham, Elias P. *Personal Narrative of Travels . . . 1817-1818,* ed. F. A. Ogg. Cleveland: A. H. Clark Co., 1906. [Length of title warrants abridgment here]

Leslie, Charles. *Histoire de la Jamaïque,* trans. Raulin. 2 vols. Londres, 1751.

Teuffel, Wilhelm Sigmund. *History of Roman Literature,* rev. & enlarg. Ludwig Schwabe; trans. George C. W. Warr. 2 vols. London: George Bell & Sons, 1900.

2. Works in a series:

The Aufère Papers: Calendar and Selections, ed. Winifred Turner. Publications of the Huguenot Society of London, No. 40. London: Frome, Butler & Tanner, 1940.

Bowers, David F., ed. *Foreign Influences in American Life:*

Essays and Critical Bibliographies. Princeton Studies in American Civilization, Vol. II. Princeton: Princeton University Press, 1944.

Judson, Alexander C. *Sidney's Appearance: A Study in Elizabethan Portraiture.* Indiana Univ. Publications, Humanities Series No. 41. Bloomington: Indiana Univ. Press, 1958.

König, Karl. *Ueberseeische Wörter im Französischen (16.-18. Jahrhundert).* Beihefte zur Zeitschrift für romanische Philologie, No. 91. Halle: Max Niemeyer Verlag, 1939. [Or, omit "Verlag"]

3. Part (chapter, essay, etc.) of a work or series:

Channing, Edward. *The Jeffersonian System, 1801-1811,* Vol. XXI of *The American Nation: A History,* ed. A. B. Hart. New York: Harper & Bros., 1906. [Essentially a separate book, though in a multivolume work, this title is italicized; cf. the next two entries]

Feise, Ernst. "Zum Problem von Goethes *Clavigo,*" *Studies in German Literature in Honor of Alexander Rudolph Hohlfeld.* Univ. of Wisconsin Studies in Language and Literature, No. 22. Madison, 1925. ["In" may be used before "*Studies.*" Page numbers are not essential, though some writers prefer to include them]

Sainte-Beuve, Charles-Augustin. "Les *Confessions* de J.-J. Rousseau," in his *Causeries du lundi,* III, 78-97. Paris: Garnier, n.d.
    Excellent analysis of originality of style of *Confessions:* naturalness, realism, occasional archaisms, and charm. (Dated Nov. 4, 1850.) [Essay in a collection; annotated entry (see also Weintraub in paragraph 7)]

4. Foreign titles:

Eslava y Elizondo, H. *Breve memoria histórica de la música religiosa en España.* Madrid, 1860.

Göpfert, Herbert Georg. "Der Dichter und das Drama unserer Zeit." *Neue Literatur,* XXXVIII (1937), 231-34.

———. *Paul Ernst und die Tragödie.* Diss., Greifswald. Leipzig, 1932. [Published; cf. Wycoco in paragraph 11]

Massini Ezcurra, José M. *El cancionero argentino*. Santa Fe, Arg., 1956. [Identification of place name added]

Mirabeau, Victor Riquetti, Marquis de. *L'Ami des hommes, ou Traité de la population*. New ed., 5 vols. Avignon, 1762.

Restori, A. "Per la storia musicale dei trovatori provenzale." *Rivista musicale italiana*, III (1896), 407-51.

Voltaire, François-Marie Arouet de. *Œuvres complètes;* ed. Moland. 52 vols. Paris: Garnier, 1877-85.

[See also Metchenko in paragraph 12]

5. Several works by one author:

Fellows, Otis E. *French Opinion of Molière (1800-1850)*. Brown Univ. Studies, Vol. III. Providence: Brown Univ., 1937.

―――. Review of *Diderot, The Testing Years, 1713-1759*, by Arthur M. Wilson. *FR*, XXXI (1958), 579-81.

―――, and Norman L. Torrey, eds. *The Age of Enlightenment: An Anthology of Eighteenth-Century French Literature*. New York: F. S. Crofts & Co., 1942. [Colon and hyphen added in title. Note that second name follows footnote style. Some authors and manuals (e.g., Chicago) prefer to give surname first]

Gwilliam, John. *The Exile of Elba: A Poem* . . . . London, [1814].

―――. *The Imperial Captive; or, The Unexampled Career of the Ex-Emperor, Napoleon* . . . . 2 vols. London, 1817.

6. Works by two or more authors: see the third entry in preceding paragraph, and Metchenko in paragraph 12.

7. Data supplied in brackets:

Benezet, Anthony. *Short Observations on Slavery, Introductory to some Extracts from the Writings of the Abbé Raynal*. . . . N.p., [1770?]. [Or, "c. 1770," in brackets]

[Fisher, Charles Edward?]. *Kanzas* [sic] *and the Constitution*. Boston: Damrell & Moore, 1856.

Schiller, Friedrich. *Werke* . . . , ed. E. Jenny. 10 vols. [Basel: Birkhäuser, 1945]. [Redundancies in titles (here, *Schillers Werke*) are usually avoided]

W[eintraub], S[tanley], ed. "St. Pancras Manifesto." *Shaw Review*, III, No. 1 (1960), 21-31.
Text of a political tract by G. B. Shaw and Sir William Geary.
[Annotated entry. Also correct: III, 1 (1960), etc.]
[See also British Museum in paragraph 9]

8. Descriptive, rather than actual, title:

Bowe, Forrest L. [Bibliographical notes on early American translations from the French]. *Papers of the Bibliographical Society of America*, XXXV (1941), 70, 72, 159-61, 205-6.
[See also the second entry in paragraph 5]

9. Institution, organization, government, etc., as author:

British Museum, Department of Printed Books. *Subject Index of the Modern Works Added to the Library of the British Museum* [1881-1935] . . . , ed. G. K. Fortescue and others. 11 vols. London, 1902-37.

Great Britain, Parliamentary Papers. *Report of the Committee of the House of Commons in Consequence of the Several Motions Relative to the Treatment of Prisoners of War* . . . . London, 1798.

Philadelphia Bibliographical Center and Union Library Catalogue. *Union List of Microfilms*. Rev. ed. Supplement, 1949-52. Ann Arbor, Mich.: J. W. Edwards, 1953.

U.S. Congress. *State Papers and Correspondence Bearing upon the Purchase of the Territory of Louisiana*. 57th Congress, 2nd sess., House Document No. 431. Washington, 1903.

10. Anonymous works:

"Daudet and Dickens." *LTLS*, May 11, 1940, p. 231. [Or, *The* (London) *Times Literary Supplement*]

H., H.S. "The 'Lost' Sixth Douay Diary." *N&Q*, CLXXVI (1944), 84-86.

Literary Amusements; Evening Entertainer. By a Female Hand. 2 vols. Dublin: S. Price and others, 1782.

Le Mari silphe, par M. F.... C.A.L.P.d.T. Musique de M.

Fournier. Toulouse: Jean Baour, 1775. [Probable interpretation: Monsieur F., collecteur à la porte de Toulouse]

11. Unpublished works:

Musa, Mark. *"Inferno,* Canto XIX." Paper read before the Renaissance Club of Indiana University, Jan. 20, 1963.

Wycoco, Remedios S. "The Types of North-American Indian Tales." Diss., Indiana Univ., May 1951.

12. Periodicals and annuals:

Cowley, Malcolm. "Footnote on French Prosody." *New Republic,* May 22, 1944, pp. 714, 716.

Henderson, W. B. Drayton. "Montaigne's *Apologie of Raymond Sebond* and *King Lear." Shakespeare Assoc. Bull.,* XIV (1939), 209-53; XV (1940), 40-54.

Metchenko, A., A. Dement'ev, and G. Lomidze. "For a Profound Elaboration of the History of Soviet Literature" ("Za glubokuyu razrabotku istorii sovetskoj literatury"). *Kommunist,* No. 13, 1956, pp. 83-100. [Translated and transliterated title. Use same form (without underlining) in translating book titles]

Muirhead, Arnold. "A Jeremy Bentham Collection." *The Library,* 5th ser., I (1947), 6-27.

Steen, J. van der. "Vondels Jempsar en de Slang." *De Nieuwe Taalgids,* LIII (1959), 326-32.

Takahashi, Atsuko. "A Study of Theodore Dreiser's Thought." *Essays and Studies in British and American Literature* (Tokyo Woman's Christian College), VII (Summer 1959), 71-102. [Model for lesser-known publications; place of origin added]

Thompson, Wade Clayton. "The Aesthetic Theory of Henry David Thoreau." *DA,* XX (1960), 3756 (Columbia). [Dissertation abstract]

13. Encyclopedias; standard reference works:

"Goldsmith, Oliver." *Encyclopaedia Britannica.* 14th ed., X, 494-98. [Or, Vol. X (omitting page numbers)]

"Gosset, Isaac." *DNB,* VIII, 261-62.

Macaulay, Thomas Babington. "Goldsmith, Oliver." *Encyclopaedia Britannica,* [etc.].

XV

PROOFREADING

112 Proofreading practices vary considerably among book and journal publishers. You will probably be asked to read galley proofs, but you may or may not get corrected galleys, page proofs, corrected page proofs, or index proofs. Your publisher will gladly tell you what his practice is. In any case, your proofs will ordinarily be read by at least one person, and sometimes more, besides yourself; but errors may still remain.

Your publisher may or may not expect you to read your proofs carefully against copy; if he does, he will return your manuscript. If he does not, you may wish to read the proofs against the copy you have retained, although this will not contain the editor's alterations. In the case of complicated or statistical material, it is advisable to hold the proof while someone else reads the copy to you. If you discover that you have little aptitude for proofreading, try to get help from someone more experienced who is familiar with your field.

You are reminded again that authors' alterations in proof can be very costly. Whether you have a formal contract or not, you will be charged according to a fixed policy. For example, you may be charged for author's alterations that exceed, say, 10 per cent of the total cost of the original typesetting. Thus if the cost of composition is $2,000, alterations in the amount of $300 will cost you $100.

The following basic procedures are recommended:

• Read slowly for sense, grammar, spelling, and punctuation.

- Read a second time, watching in particular for the more elusive typographical errors, faulty spacing, etc. Complex parts such as footnotes and bibliography require special attention, and a separate scrutiny of alignment (e.g., of numbers, periods, indentions, margins), word division, and quotations in a foreign language will often reveal errors.

- Answer all editor's queries.

- Insert conventional proofreaders' marks (see specimen pages 4, 5) in margin opposite the error, separating multiple marks by slant lines. Avoid arrows and unconventional symbols. Guide lines are used only when corrections are overcrowded, and should never cross one another. It is a good idea to indicate printer's errors in one color pencil, your own alterations in another. To assure legibility, print your own corrections or write them very clearly.

- Contrary to the directions for making alterations in the manuscript, *all* corrections on proof should be written *in the margin*. In the type line, indicate only where the correction is to be made. In correcting proof, the compositor does not read the text; he merely casts his eye down the margin to note where corrections must be made. Hence a correction written into the body of the text will probably escape his attention.

- Indicate with a caret below the line the exact place where an addition (extra space, missing words or punctuation, etc.) is to be made. Correct only what is wrong (e.g., delete a single incorrect letter rather than the entire word). If an entire word is deleted, draw a horizontal line through it and write a delete mark in the margin. To delete one character, draw a vertical line through it and write the delete mark in the margin. If necessary to close space after deletion, show this in the margin (⌒) and in the correction (e.g., lost). Numbers and abbreviations that should be spelled out, letters to be transposed, and broken type should be circled; but do not mark characters where uneven inking has caused a slight fading (e.g., in the tail of a *y*), or passages that appear muddy, as sometimes happens in galley proofs.

• To retain an occasional word deleted in error, it suffices to cross out the delete mark in the margin. To retain a long passage, cross out the delete mark and write in the margin (circled) "don't change," "OK as printed," or "stet."

• To fill a gap caused by a deletion, try to substitute something of equal length (an equal number of letters and spaces), placed in the same or a nearby line. If a few words are added, try to delete copy of equal length. This will avoid the possible resetting of several lines following —an added expense and an invitation to new errors.

• If you make any extensive insertions on proof (i.e., more than a line or two that can easily be written on the galley itself), type the inserts on separate pages (several can go on one page), each clearly marked, e.g., "Insert A, galley 56," with an indication on galley 56, "Insert A here." Return these pages with the proof but not attached to the galley in question.

• If one or more lines of copy are missing, write "see copy" (circled) in margin and show point of insertion with a caret.

• If you are checking corrected proofs, read the entire line in which a correction has been made to catch any new error that may have crept in. Also, inspect the line above and the line below to see if the corrected line has been inserted in its proper place.

- Return proof sheets promptly, together with editor's manuscript copy if this has been sent to you.

113 Word division at ends of lines demands the proofreader's close attention notwithstanding that compositors in general handle it (at least as regards English words) with considerable skill. The particulars in the following sections are furnished for convenient reference.

114 English words are divided as follows:

1. In the United States (but not in Great Britain) the division is primarily on the basis of sound: the pronunciation of the line-end fragment must be compatible with that of the whole word. Thus syllabication will often be at variance with etymology: *finan-cier, bibliog-raphy, philol-ogy, personae, ambig-uous, prec-ipice, chil-dren.*

2. They may, however, divide in accordance with etymology, meaning, and sound: *biblio-phile, philo-logical, person-ify, ambi-guity, pre-fix, child-ish.*

3. Words sometimes divide immediately before a suffix (*wish-ing, judg-ment, blu-ish, hum-ble, social-ism*), sometimes not (*tack-ling, stop-ping, tick-lish, witti-cism, sati-rist*).

4. Double like consonants usually divide (*Rus-sian, difficult*), but not always (*dress-ing, dull-ard, all-over, passably*).

For further refinements, see the Chicago *Manual of Style.* When in doubt about syllabication, consult any of the latest dictionaries.

115 French words are divided as follows:

1. A single consonant between vowels (including the nasalized vowels *an, en, in, on, un,* etc.) goes with the following syllable: *co-mé-die, a-mou-reux, cir-con-ven-tion, main-te-nant.*

2. Double consonants usually divide: *bail-lant, bap-tême, tor-til-lage;* but two unlike consonants, the second of which is

l or *r*, belong with the following syllable: *éta-blir, pro-créer, peu-ple*. Exceptions are *rl* and *lr*, which always divide: *par-ler, mer-luche, Mal-raux*.

3. Two consonants representing one sound do not divide: *tou-cher, or-phi-que, mono-thé-isme*.

4. The commonplace liquid sound *gn* is never divided (*ma-gni-fique, monta-gne*), but in certain less commonly used words of learned or foreign origin these consonants are divided: *diag-nostique, stag-nation, reg-nicole*, etc.

116 Italian words are divided as follows:

1. A single consonant between vowels goes with the following syllable: *do-ma-ni, li-be-ra-to-re*.

2. Double like consonants are divided: *repub-blica, at-tiz-zamento*.

3. Two consonants, the first of which is *l, m, n*, or *r*, are divided: *al-bero, lam-pada, man-dare, por-porato*.

4. Other combinations of two consonants go with the following syllable: *da-gli, antipa-sto, monta-gne, chiaro-scuro;* but consonants that cannot be pronounced together are divided: *prag-matismo, op-tare, seg-mento, dog-matico*.

5. The first of three consonants, except *s*, goes with the preceding syllable: *com-prare, Lon-dra, sem-preverde, chiac-chierare;* but *di-stributivo, e-straneo*.

6. Diphthongs containing an unstressed *i* or *u* are never divided: *giu-sto, gio-varsi, uo-mini, Eu-ropa, princi-pio*. (Certain vowel combinations can divide because they are not true diphthongs: *pa-esano, co-eterno*.)

117 Spanish words are divided as follows:

1. A word has as many syllables as it has vowels or diphthongs: *ba-úl, an-ti-ci-par-se, o-pe-ra-cio-nes, ca-lien-te*.

2. A single consonant between vowels goes with the following syllable: *i-ma-gi-na-ble, a-le-mán, espa-ñol*.

3. *ch*, *ll*, and *rr* go with the following syllable: *le-che, ta-llador, papa-rrucha*.

4. Two consonants between vowels usually divide: *ac-ción, in-negable, nin-guno, os-ten-toso, or-nato*.

5. *l* and *r* go with a preceding consonant: *a-blan-dar, re-trac-tación, fil-tración;* but prepositional prefixes form separate syllables: *sub-lunar, des-re-glado, a-climatar*.

6. In the combination *s* plus a consonant, the *s* goes with the preceding syllable, prefix or not: *es-labón, abs-tener*.

118 German words are divided as follows:

1. A single consonant and groups of consonants which represent single sounds (*ch, sch, ph, th, st*) go with the following syllable: *Li-te-ra-tur, Mär-chen, Spre-cher, For-schung, Stro-phen, ka-tholisch, Mei-ster*.

2. Other consonant groups are usually divided: *Hun-ger, ir-gend, im-mer, interes-sieren*.

3. If *ck* is divided, spelling changes to *k-k*: *stückeln—stük-keln. Tz* is divided *t-z*: *blit-zen*.

4. Compound words are divided into their component parts: *Ver-ein, Manu-script, Falsch-heit, blut-rot, ehr-bar*.

5. In foreign words, *b, d, g, k, p, t* plus *l* or *r* are carried over: *Pu-blikum, Me-trum, Ma-krone*.

119 Russian words. Russian and other Slavic words (including transliterations.) divide in an involved manner that can best be explained by a person conversant with them.

120 Latin words are divided as follows:

1. A consonant between vowels goes with the following syllable (*pe-cu-nia, fi-gu-ra*) except when there is a compounding juncture present: *ab-orior, prod-eo, per-inde*.

2. Double consonants usually divide: *tris-tis, bel-lum;* but *b, p, d, t, g, c, ch, ph, th* plus *l* or *r* are carried over: *pa-tribus, ne-glectum, mi-thrax, a-phron*.

3. When there are more than two consonants between vowels, all but the first go with the following syllable (*mon-strum, claus-tra*) except when there is a compounding juncture present: *trans-gressus, post-habeo*. Words containing the combination *l, m, n, r* plus *ct, ps, pt* are sometimes divided between the second and third letters: *consump-tus, farc-tus*.

4. Two contiguous vowels or a vowel and a diphthong can be divided: *the-atrum, de-aeque*.

121 Greek words divide according to the same general principles as do Latin words.

FOR REFERENCE

Additional titles in the categories below can readily be found in library catalogues and in the latest issues of *Cumulative Book Index* (New York: H. W. Wilson); *Subject Guide to "Books in Print": An Index to the "Publishers' Trade List Annual"* (New York: R. R. Bowker); *Library of Congress Catalog. Books: Subjects* (Washington: Library of Congress); *Scientific, Medical, and Technical Books Published in the United States of America* (Washington: National Academy of Sciences), and other current bibliographies. Books listed below, with the exception of the new edition of Porter G. Perrin, were in print in 1964.

PUBLISHING (GENERAL)

Gill, Robert J. *Author—Publisher—Printer Complex.* 3d ed. Baltimore: Williams & Wilkins, 1960.

Literary Market Place: The Directory of American Book Publishing. New York: R. R. Bowker, 1964-65. (Revised annually.)

Welter, Rush. *Problems of Scholarly Publication in the Humanities and Social Sciences.* New York: American Council of Learned Societies, 1959.

STYLING; MANUSCRIPT PREPARATION

"American Journals in the Humanities: A Guide to Scope and Editorial Policy." *PMLA*, LXXII, No. 4, Pt. 2 (1957), 52-65.

Bowers, Fredson. *Principles of Bibliographical Description.* New York: Russell & Russell, 1962.

Byrd, Milton B., and Arnold L. Goldsmith. *Publication Guide* [to over 180 journals] *for Literary and Linguistic Scholars.* Detroit: Wayne State University Press, 1958.

Collins, Frederick H. *Authors' and Printers' Dictionary: A Guide for Authors, Editors, Printers, Correctors of the Press, Compositors, and Typists.* 10th ed. New York: Oxford University Press, 1956.

Collison, Robert L. *Indexing Books: A Manual of Basic Principles.* New York: DeGraff, 1962.

Fieser, Louis F., and Mary Fieser. *Style Guide for Chemists.* New York: Reinhold, 1960.

Fishbein, Morris. *Medical Writing: The Technic and the Art.* 3rd ed. New York: McGraw-Hill, 1957.

Handbook for Chemical Society Authors. Chemical Society Special Publication No. 14. London: The Chemical Society, 1960.

Lasky, Joseph. *Proofreading and Copy-Preparation: A Textbook for the Graphic Arts Industry.* New York: Mentor Press, 1954.

The MLA Style Sheet, comp. William Riley Parker. Rev. ed. New York: Modern Language Association of America, 1964.

McKerrow, Ronald B. "Form and Matter in the Publication of Research." *Review of English Studies,* XVI (1940), 116-21; reprinted in *PMLA,* LXV, No. 3 (1950), 3-8.

―――. *An Introduction to Bibliography for Literary Students.* Oxford: Clarendon Press, 1928.

A Manual of Style. 11th ed., rev. Chicago: University of Chicago Press, 1949.

A Manual of Style for the "Astrophysical Journal." Chicago: University of Chicago Press, 1955.

"A Manual for Authors of Mathematical Papers." *Bulletin of the American Mathematical Society,* LXVIII (1962), 429-44. Later offprints available.

NEA Style Manual for Writers and Editors. Washington: National Education Association, 1962.

Publication Manual of the American Psychological Association. Washington: American Psychological Association, 1957.

Skillen, Marjorie E., and Robert M. Gay. *Words into Type: A Guide in the Preparation of Manuscripts, for Writers, Editors, Proofreaders, and Printers*. Rev. ed. Des Moines, Iowa: Meredith, 1964.

Spiker, Sina. *Indexing Your Book. A Practical Guide for Authors*. Madison: University of Wisconsin Press, 1964.

Style Manual for Biological Journals. 2nd ed. Washington: American Institute of Biological Sciences, 1964.

Style Manual for Guidance in the Preparation of Papers for Journals Published by the American Institute of Physics. 2nd ed. New York: American Institute of Physics, 1959. (Used also in the field of astronomy.)

U.S.—Geological Survey. *Suggestions to Authors of the Reports of the United States Geological Survey*. 5th ed. Washington: Government Printing Office, 1958.

A Uniform System of Citation. 10th ed. Cambridge: The Harvard Law Review Association, 1964.

Wiles, Roy M. *Scholarly Reporting in the Humanities*. 3rd ed. Toronto: University of Toronto Press, 1961.

GRAPHS; STATISTICS

Conway, Frieda. *Descriptive Statistics*. Leicester: Leicester University Press, 1963.

Croxton, Frederick E., and D. J. Cowden. *Applied General Statistics*. 2nd ed. New York: Prentice-Hall, 1960.

Myers, John H. *Statistical Presentation*. Ames, Iowa: Littlefield, Adams, 1956.

Spear, Mary E. *Charting Statistics*. New York: McGraw-Hill, 1952.

ILLUSTRATION

Gibby, Joseph C. *Technical Illustration*. Chicago: American Technical Society, 1962.

Thomas, T. A. *Technical Illustration*. New York: McGraw-Hill, 1960.

COPYRIGHT PRACTICE

Nicholson, Margaret. *A Manual of Copyright Practice for Writers, Publishers, and Agents*. 2nd ed. New York: Oxford University Press, 1956.

Pilpel, Harriet F., and Morton D. Goldberg. *A Copyright Guide*. 2nd ed. New York: R. R. Bowker, 1963.

Pilpel, Harriet F., and Theodora S. Zavin. *Rights and Writers. A Handbook of Literary and Entertainment Law*. New York: E. P. Dutton, 1960.

AIDS TO WRITERS

A. General

Baker, Sheridan. "Are You Communicating?" *Bulletin of the American Association of University Professors*, XXXIX (1953), 432-37.

———. "Scholarly Style, or the Lack Thereof." Ibid., XLII (1956), 464-70.

Barzun, Jacques, and Henry F. Graff. *The Modern Researcher*. New York: Harcourt, Brace & World, 1957; Harbinger Books, 1962. (Field: history; see Part III: "Writing.")

Brittain, Robert E. *Punctuation; an Easy Method of Learning to Punctuate Correctly*. Everyday Handbook. New York: Barnes & Noble, 1955.

Copperud, Ray H. *Words on Paper: A Manual of Prose Style for Professional Writers, Reporters, Authors, Editors, Publishers, and Teachers*. New York: Hawthorn Books, 1960.

Evans, Bergen, and Cornelia Evans. *A Dictionary of Contemporary American Usage*. New York: Random House, 1957.

Fowler, Henry W. *A Dictionary of Modern English Usage*. Rev. ed. Oxford: Clarendon Press, 1960.

————, and F. G. Fowler. *The King's English*. 3rd ed. Oxford: Clarendon Press, 1958.

Goodman, Roger B. *A Concise Handbook of Better English*. Bantam Reference Library. New York: Bantam Books, 1962.

Gorrell, Robert M., and Charlton Laird. *Modern English Handbook*. 3rd ed. Englewood Cliffs, N.J.: Prentice-Hall, 1962.

Graves, Robert, and Alan Hodge. *The Reader Over Your Shoulder: A Handbook for Writers of English Prose*. New York: Macmillan, 1961.

Hook, Julius N. *Guide to Good Writing: Grammar, Style, Usage*. New York: Ronald Press, 1962.

————, and E. G. Mathews. *Modern American Grammar and Usage*. New York: Ronald Press, 1956.

Horwill, Herbert W. *A Dictionary of Modern American Usage*. 2nd ed. Oxford: Clarendon Press, 1958.

Ives, Sumner. *A New Handbook for Writers*. New York: Knopf, 1962.

Kent, Sherman. *Writing History*. New York: Appleton-Century-Crofts, 1954.

Nicholson, Margaret. *Dictionary of American-English Usage*. New York: Oxford University Press, 1957.

Perrin, Porter G., Karl W. Dykema, and Wilma E. Ebbitt. *Writer's Guide and Index to English*. 4th ed. Chicago: Scott, Foresman, 1965.

Shaw, Harry. *Punctuate It Right!* Everyday Handbook. New York: Barnes & Noble, 1963.

Sillen, Samuel. *Standard Handbook of Style*. New York: Grosset & Dunlap, 1963.

Summey, George, Jr. *American Punctuation*. New York: Ronald Press, 1949.

Whitford, Robert C., and James R. Foster. *Dictionary of American Grammar and Usage*. Littlefield College Outlines. Ames, Iowa: Littlefield, Adams, 1957.

B. Technical and Scientific Writing

Blickle, Margaret D., and Kenneth W. Houp. *Reports for Science and Industry*. New York: Holt, 1958.

Crouch, W. George, and Robert L. Zetler. *A Guide to Technical Writing*. 3rd ed. New York: Ronald Press, 1964.

Emberger, Meta R., and Marian R. Hall. *Scientific Writing*. New York: Harcourt, Brace, 1955.

Estrin, Herman A. *Technical and Professional Writing*. New York: Harcourt, Brace & World, 1963.

Norgaard, Margaret. *A Technical Writer's Handbook, for Technicians, Engineers, Educators, Businessmen, and Scientists*. New York: Harper, 1959.

Peterson, Martin S. *Scientific Thinking and Scientific Writing*. New York: Reinhold, 1961.

Rathbone, Robert R., and James B. Stone. *A Writer's Guide for Engineers and Scientists*. Englewood Cliffs, N.J.: Prentice-Hall, 1962.

Roberts, Ffrangcon. *Good English for Medical Writers*. Springfield, Ill.: Charles C. Thomas, 1960.

Sherman, Theodore A. *Modern Technical Writing*. New York: Prentice-Hall, 1955.

Trelease, Sam F. *How to Write Scientific and Technical Papers*. Baltimore: Williams & Wilkins, 1958.

Wellborn, G. P., L. B. Green, and K. A. Nall. *Technical Writing*. Boston: Houghton Mifflin, 1961.

Writing in Industry, ed. Siegfried Mandel. Vol. I. Brooklyn, N.Y.: Plenum Press, 1959.

SPECIMEN PAGE 1

Corrected Typescript

31

descendants of Logan--*a* family, through intermar*r*iage, "neither
Indian nor white, neither savage nor civilized." ¶A four-act
play, <u>Logan</u>: <u>The</u> <u>Last</u> <u>of</u> <u>the</u> <u>Race</u> <u>of</u> <u>Shikellemus</u>, <u>Chief</u> <u>of</u>
<u>the Cayuga Nation</u>, was published by Dr. Joseph Doddridge at
Buffaloe Creek, Virginia, in 1823. Based on the familiar
background of the delivery of the speech, it closes with
Logan reading his message to Lord Dunmore from "a belt of
white wampum." Joseph D. Canning's two poems, "The Shade
of Logan" and "Epitaph for the Logan Monument," were pub-
lished in Williams' <u>American</u> <u>Pioneer</u> (March 1842, October 1843).
~~The first, containing fourteen quatrains, includes a paraphrase~~
~~of Logan's speech.~~ Both ~~pieces~~ *poems* were reprinted as an appendix
to later editions of Doddridge's play, <u>Logan</u>. Fairchild points
out in <u>The</u> <u>Noble</u> <u>Savage</u> (pp. 276) that William Lisle Bowles
acknowledges an obvious debt to Logan for the words spoken by
his warrior Caupolican: "Who shall be there to mourn for me?
--Not one!" The poem in question is "The Missionary" (Canto
I, ℓ. 203), published in <u>The Poetical Works of William Lisle</u>
<u>Bowles</u> (Edinburgh, 1855) a similar borrowing is found in Henry
Rowe Schoolcraft's poem "<u>Geehale</u>: an Indian Lament," which
ends:

> My wife and my children, O, spare me the tale!
> For tho is there left that is kin to Geehale?

83

SPECIMEN PAGE 2

Typescript That Need Not Be Recopied

analogous (insert p. 25a)

Guillon himself related two examples.[45] Lamartine, in a letter of 1810, ~~exclaimed~~: "Voici l'automne: c'est le temps où
je deviens amoureux, mélancolique, rêveur, ennuyé de la vie;
c'est le temps où je lis Werther, et où je suis souvent tenté
d'imiter cet aimable et malheureux héros de roman";[46] and
Auguste Sautelet wrote to his friend Sainte-Beuve:

"Tu ne sais pas la mauvaise pensée qui me vient à l'in-
stant! c'est que je voudrais me brûler la cervelle pour
terminer mes doutes. Si, dans une année ou deux, la vie
ne me paraît pas claire, j'y mettrai fin. J'exécuterai
cette idée que j'ai eue de mon Werther de la vérité."[47]

~~Common knowledge that suicide is apparently contagious~~
also led to the reaction against Werther. Cases of "heredi-
tary" suicide have been known in every community, and notori-
ous examples of mass suicide have been recorded since the
pre-Christian era.[48] Those accomplished by jumping from the
Colonne de Juillet, the Arc de Triomphe, or the towers of
Notre Dame were alone enough to support the notion that a
story as impelling ~~as Werther might well set off a train of
self-destruction.~~ ¶ That ~~Goethe's novel~~ Werther was considered
a potential danger is (also/seen) in the appearance of antidotes
like Werther, ou les Egarements d'un coeur sensible, a parody
by Duval and Rochefort, hailed by the Journal des Débats
(october 6, 1817) as a useful device for ridiculing the "détestable frénésie" of suicide sweeping over France.[48] The

←——— Guillon himself related two ^analogous examples. [46] Lamartine, in a letter ~~to a friend, exclaimed~~ ^of 1810: "Voici | | | ^le temps où je deviens amoureux, mélancolique, rêveur, ennuyé de la vie; c'est le temps où je lis _Werther_, et où je suis souvent tenté d'imiter cet aimable et malheureux héros de roman";[46] and Auguste Sautelet wrote to his friend Saint^e-Beuve:

"Tu ne sais pas la mauvaise pensée qui me vient à l'in-
stant! c'est que je voudrais me brûler la cervelle pour
terminer mes doutes. Si, dans une année ou deux, la vie
ne me paraît pas claire, j'y mettrai fin, j'exécuterai cette
idée que j'ai eue de mon _Werther de la vérité_."[47]

¶ ~~Some writers have, of course, made light of the attri-~~ That ~~Goethe's novel~~ _Werther_ was considered a potential dan-
ger ~~and a baleful influence~~ is (also seen) in the appearance of an^tidotes like _Werther, ou les egarements d'un coeur sensible_, a parody by Duval, ~~mentioned~~ ^and Rochefort by the _Journal des Débats_ (6 October 1817) as a useful device (hailed) ^for ridiculing the "détestable frénésie" of suicide sweeping over France.[48] Literature ~~that~~ condon^ing ~~ed~~ suicide was ~~of course~~ no novelty, to ^be sure, to the well-read Frenchman of the late (18th) century: he was familiar with the Greco-Roman ^Apologists, whose ideas sur-
vived in the works of Montaigne, the Abbé de Saint-Cyran, Helvétius, Delisle de Sales, Voltaire, and Rousseau, and, in England, Donne, Blount, Gildon, and Hume. But Werther ~~was~~ ^stood

The general alarm over Goethe's novel was vigorous enough to outlive the nineteenth century;[49] it may have been, in a sense, groundless, yet it was patently sincere and, for several reasons, inevitable.

SPECIMEN PAGE 4

Proofreaders' Marks

ℓ	Delete	❛❛ ❜❜	Insert double quotes
⊂	Close up	=	Insert hyphen
ℓ͡	Delete & close up	1/M	Insert em dash
#	Insert space	?	Insert interrogation mark
cap	Set in capital(s)	e 2	Insert superior letter, figure, etc.
sc	Set in small capitals	a 2	Insert inferior letter, figure, etc.
lc	Set in lower case	||	Align type
bf	Set in bold face	=	Straighten line
ital	Set in italics	[	Move to left
rom	Set in roman	]	Move to right
stet	Let it stand	⊔	Lower
tr	Transpose	⊓	Raise
sp	Spell out	9	Reverse (e.g., an inverted letter)
⁀	Ligature	wf	Wrong font
n/2/he	Insert, at caret	X	Broken type
⊙	Insert period	∧∨	Space evenly
:	Insert colon	¶	Paragraph
^,	Insert comma	no ¶	No paragraph
;	Insert semicolon		
❜ ❛	Insert apostrophe or single quote		

Corrected Galley Proof

The frigates and warships remain at Port Royal.
At the time there were five of them there, one
of which, with two decks, was the flagship of
the *Blue-Squadron*, now in these parts. A
frigate formerly taken from the French bears
the name The Active and is reputed one of the
fastest English boats. The English greatly ad-
mire our construction; of this we are only too
well aware.

After long suffering from the conceit of several officers who came aboard to inspect us,
and particularly that of a chief customs officer,
who was quite as haughty and impertinent as
those of France, and after enduring a quantity
of questions, we went ashore.

I have the honor, etc.

Letter IX

Kingston, March 15, 1817.

It is not without difficulty that I have established myself in this city; indeed, it appears that
the English, these great preachers of liberty,
reserve it for themselves. You cannot imagine
the objections they raised in granting me a
needed letters of introduction, and the offer I
made to deposit close to 10 thousand francs that
I had brought along piqued them without
altering their opinion. After my traveling com-

line out, see copy

INDEX

Unless otherwise indicated, references are to numbered sections rather than to page numbers.

Plays—*Cont.*
   titles of, how cited, 43
Poems
   bibliographical data omitted, 60, 82
   ellipsis in, 61
   in footnotes, how cited, 70
   line numbers, how used, 60
   parenthetical source references to, 60
   titles of, how cited, 43, 44, 87
   how typed, 60, 70
Possessives, how written, 41
Preface
   contents of, 23
   placement of, 21
Proofreading
   example of, specimen page 5
   marks used in, specimen page 4
   technique of, 112
Proper names, *see* Initials; Names, proper
Prose quotations
   capitalization in, 57
   in footnotes, how typed, 69
   italics in, 58
   paragraphing in, 62
   parenthetical source references in, 59
   how typed, 55, 56, 69
   see also Ellipsis
Pseudonymous works, how cited, 72, 103, 104
Publishers' names
   how cited, 82, 84
   omission of, 82, 84
Publishers' requirements, 1

Quotation marks
   double, 37, 69
   foreign, 37
   punctuation with, 37
   single, 37
Quoted matter
   accuracy in, 10
   how typed, 55, 56, 69, 70
   see also Poems; Prose quotations; Copyrighted material

Reference indexes, *see* Footnote references in text
Reviews, how cited, 111 par. 5
Revision of manuscript, *see* Manuscript, author's
Russian, word division in, 119

Secondary sources, how cited, 97 n. 26
ser., 86, 95
Series title, how cited, 45, 80
sic
   avoidance of, 33, 39 n.
   use of, 39 n., 43
   how written, 39
Sideheads, 29
Spacing in typescript, 19, 56, 70
Spanish
   ellipsis in, 61
   proper names, how written, 51, 74, 107
   titles, capitalization of, 48
   word division in, 117
Spelling
   anomalies in, how treated, 7
   consistency in, 4, 8